Scrapbooking Life's Celebrations

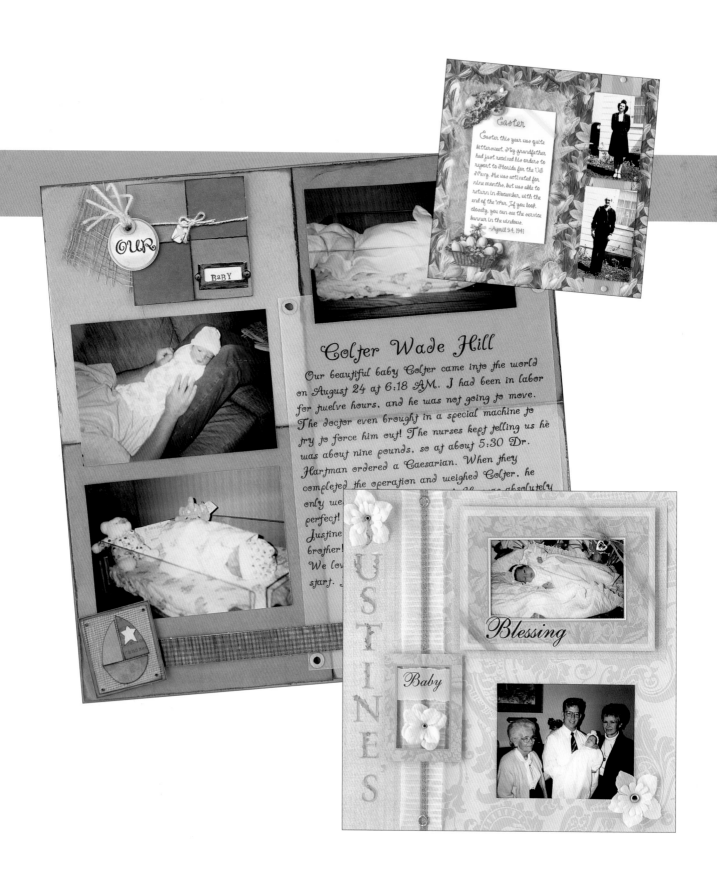

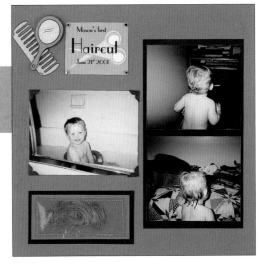

Scrapbooking Life's Celebrations

200 Page Designs

PAIGE HILL

Sterling Publication Co., Inc. New York
A Sterling/Chapelle Book

CHAPELLE, LTD.:

Jo Packham, Sara Toliver, Cindy Stoeckl

If you have any questions or comments, please contact:

Chapelle, Ltd., Inc.,
P.O. Box 9252 Ogden, UT 84409
(801) 621-2777
(801) 621-2788 Fax
e-mail: chapelle@chapelleltd.com
Web site: www.chapelleltd.com

Library of Congress Cataloging-in-Publication Data
Hill, Paige.
Scrapbooking life's celebrations : 200 page designs / Paige Hill.
    p. cm.
Includes index.
ISBN 1-4027-1392-4
1. Photograph albums. 2. Photographs–Conservation and restoration. 3. Scrapbooks. I. Title.
TR465.H55 2005
745.593–dc22
                            2004016217

10 9 8 7 6 5 4 3 2 1
Published by Sterling Publishing Co., Inc.
387 Park Avenue South, New York, NY 10016
©2005 by Paige Hill
Distributed in Canada by Sterling Publishing
c/o Manda Group, 165 Dufferin Street
Toronto, Ontario, Canada M6K 3H6
Distributed in Great Britain by Chrysalis Books Group PLC, The Chrysalis Building, Bramley Road, London W10 6SP, England
Distributed in Australia by Capricorn Link (Australia) Pty. Ltd.
P. O. Box 704, Windsor, NSW 2756, Australia
Printed and Bound in China
All Rights Reserved

Sterling ISBN 1-4027-1392-4

Dedication

This book is dedicated to the memory of my beloved father, Val Wayment, who taught me to believe in myself and always encouraged me to explore my creativity. I love you Dad!

CONTENTS

Legacy

A legacy is something you leave for future generations to remember you by. Three years ago, my mother gave me a precious gift—my grandmother's old scrapbook. I spent an entire weekend going through my wonderful treasure. My time with my grandparents was short: my grandfather died when I was just seven and my grandmother when I was fifteen. I felt so lucky that I could learn about their early years together.

I knew I had to save these precious artifacts for future generations, so I researched the best way to preserve old photographs, newspaper clippings, and other important items. I copied everything and stored them on my computer. I keep originals in acid-free boxes and albums.

I also wanted to research more of what I had begun to learn, so I headed to the library. I learned so much about my family, the nation, our state, and the city we all grew up in. For instance, on the day my grandfather was born, February 11, 1919, the headlines read "Senate Votes on Suffrage" and "World Pays Tribute to Theodore Roosevelt." When my grandmother was born, you could by a T-bone steak for twenty-five cents a pound! Going through those old reels helped me to understand the way of life back then, and I also learned how important it is to leave this kind of legacy for my own children. It's for this reason that this book is written.

General Instructions

In addition to the papers, die-cuts, stickers, and other accents needed to create your scrapbook pages, you will need some basic supplies to have on hand. Here is a list of tools you will need:

- Archival adhesive (of choice)
- Craft knife
- Eyelet-setting tool
- Fine-grit sandpaper
- Flat-head screwdriver
- Medium paintbrush
- Paper-piercing tool or awl
- Pencil
- Ruler
- Scissors
- Water
- Wire cutters

ADHESIVES

There are a variety of adhesives generally used in scrapbooking. Ranging from liquid glues to roll-tape adhesives it can be overwhelming to say the least. So where should you start? First, make sure the adhesives you choose are acid-free, making them safe for photographs. Not all adhesives are acid-free, so check the labels. Next, what are the jobs at hand? To adhere photographs, roll-tape dispensers are both quick and easy to use. They come in different styles, some with photo tabs, and some with double-sided tape. These adhesives are also either permanent or repositional, which is great when you're indecisive about photograph placement. Liquid glues are great for die-cuts and other small accents. Most are double duty; meaning that they are permanent when wet, but when

allowed to dry slightly, will be repositional. Glue dots are small adhesive dots, great for attaching metal elements, buttons, and other items that liquid glues won't hold. Foam tape, dots, or squares are a great way to make items "stand out" on your pages. They are available in different thicknesses, so if you don't want a lot of bulk, pick the thinnest.

CHALK PASTELS

Chalks are used to blend and/or shade around journaling, torn paper, photographs, or other accents. Generally they are available in palette form, with a variety of colors. To apply chalk, use a small sponge-tipped applicator, cotton swabs, or even your finger. Rub gently, a little goes a long way. You can soften the effect by brushing with a cotton ball. Chalk pastels are acid-free, nontoxic, and add an artistic touch to your pages.

COMPUTER FONTS

Journaling is one of the most important elements of your page. Imagine future generations looking to you to tell them what you were feeling at that particular time. With this in mind, be sure to include who, what, where, when, and why. Your story is important. Your family and friends will want to read about it, so use your best penmanship.

What if your handwriting is less than perfect? That's where your computer comes in. There are literally thousands of different fonts available for your use; all you need is a word processing program, printer,

and access to the Internet. Simply type the words "free fonts" in your search engine, and download as many as you like.

If you don't have Internet access, or aren't computer savvy, that's ok. Most word processing programs have hundreds of fonts already installed for your use, and are very user friendly. Another option is to buy a font CD, which will install the fonts directly to your computer. These are available at craft stores, office supply stores, and bookstores.

You don't need an expensive printer, just a simple ink-jet is fine. Most printers accept just about any type of paper; but be aware that vellum and transparencies may need a different setting so as to not smudge the ink. Check the manual or word processing program to be sure.

Computer journaling is easy once you get the hang of it; but if you prefer handwriting your journaling, that's ok too. It's all about your personal preference.

CROPPING PHOTOGRAPHS

If we were all fabulous photographers, we probably wouldn't need to crop. However the truth is, even if you are a fabulous photographer, there probably are elements in your photograph you don't need. Just be certain the item you crop isn't something that will be important to someone. For example, you may be tempted to crop some of the toys or clutter from a Christmas morning photograph; but think ahead—won't your children want to remember how

everything looked on that special morning? Keep this in mind. Focus on your subject but be selective of what you crop.

So how do you crop? Simply use a paper trimmer to make a clean, sharp edge. If you choose to mat your photograph, cut your mat in the same fashion. Remember: never crop an original photograph. Always cut from photocopies. You might want to remember what that oak tree looked like in your front yard, before you cropped it out of the birthday party picture.

CURLING WIRE

Wire can be used as an embellishment on your scrapbook page. Simply twist the wire around the end of a pencil. When the wire is fastened to the page, curl any loose ends. This will give it a decorative curl which will enhance the layout.

EYELET TOOLS

Eyelets are great accents for your pages. They come in many different sizes, shapes, and colors; so you're sure to find something to fit your needs. Of course, you'll need tools to punch and set the eyelet. The first tool you will need is a self-healing mat. This is a necessity, as you don't want to ruin your workspace with eyelet holes.

Next, you will need an "anywhere" punch, hammer, and an eyelet setter. If you plan on using different sizes of eyelets, it makes sense to purchase a punch and setter that have interchangeable heads to fit the eyelet of your choice. To set eyelets, mark your placement with a pencil and place the self-healing mat under the spot. Next, place the punch over the pencil spot, and lightly tap with the hammer. Place the eyelet in the hole, turn the paper over, place the eyelet setter in the back of the eyelet, and lightly tap with the hammer.

PAPER-PIERCING TOOL

Before sewing or setting brads through delicate paper, pierce a hole in the desired location. This technique will help in not tearing or creasing the paper in your layout and will give your page a more professional appearance.

PHOTOGRAPHS

Always use photocopies in your scrapbooks. Keep the originals separate in acid-free photo boxes or albums. Even though you use acid-free items in scrapbooks, you should always have another copy, just in case. No matter how careful you are, accidents can happen; so always use photocopies.

Another great idea is to keep your photographs catalogued on a CD. If you can't, most photo processors can do it for a nominal fee. It's a good investment to be able to have years of photographs right at your fingertips.

SANDING & DISTRESSING PAPER

Occasionally, you might want a more "vintage" look to your layout. Maybe the paper you have is a little too contemporary, or you just want a different feel—distressing is easy! Using a fine-grade sandpaper, lightly (or heavily, depending on your taste) sand your paper, die-cut, or accent.

For a truly vintage look, crumple your paper before you sand, then apply brown pastel chalk to the creases in the paper.

TEARING PAPER

Simply tear the paper, using your fingers as a guide. You can tear in waves, or straight lines. Another more controlled way to tear paper is by using a deckle-edged ruler. Use like a measuring ruler, but instead of marking, tear the lines away. Chalk the torn edges if you prefer.

To tear mulberry paper, trace the area you want torn with a wet paintbrush. Tear along the dampened area.

USING RIBBON

Secure the ribbon ends to the back side of the layout with acid-free tape. Be certain not to use cellophane tape, as it is not acid-free. You can also adhere or even stitch the ribbon on, depending on your preference.

We're Having a Baby

BACKGROUND PAPER:

Yellow swirl patterned

LAYOUT PAPER:

Purple checkered

SUPPLIES:

½"-square stitched metal tile

Adhesive foam dots

Baby announcement

Brads: lavender, mini silver

Clear vellum

Mini lavender eyelets

Paper crimper

Personal letter

Ribbons: ⅛"-wide white silk,
¼"-wide purple organdy

Small rectangle punch

Stickers: alphabet, daisy

DETAILS:

- (above right) To make the journaling pocket, cut a 4¾"x7½" piece and an 8"x1" strip from the checkered paper. Adhere the larger piece on the bottom-right corner of the first page.

- Cut a 4¾"x5¼" piece from the journaled vellum, making sure the journaling is centered.

- Make an accordion fold in the strip of patterned paper.

- Secure all pieces in place with the mini silver brads.

Once Upon a Time . . .

BACKGROUND PAPER:
Blue & pink plaid patterned

LAYOUT PAPER:
Storybook patterned

SUPPLIES:
¼"-wide green gingham ribbon
Adhesive foam dots
Clear vellum
Light green embossed paper
Light green mulberry paper
Mini gold brads
Star nail heads
Storybook stickers

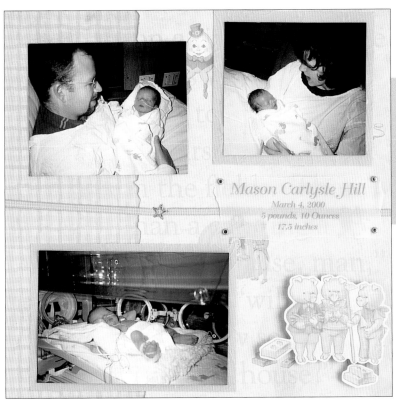

DETAILS:
- Mat photographs onto the embossed paper as desired.
- Frame one matted photograph with a torn piece of mulberry paper.

Justine Helen Hill

BACKGROUND PAPER:

Pink floral patterned

SUPPLIES:

2½"x4" Victorian-style decorative tag

Adhesive foam dots

Heart button

Pink cardstock

Pink thread

Ribbons: ⅝"-wide green & pink hand-dyed silk, 1½"-wide pink sinamay

Rose die-cuts

Rose stickers

DETAILS:

• To make borders for the page, place pieces of sinamay ribbon on the top and bottom edges of the page.

• Using a zigzag stitch, sew the pieces to the page. (Refer to Stitches Guide on page 126.)

TIP To eliminate bulk, remove the shank from the heart button with wire cutters.

Kaira's Birth

BACKGROUND PAPER:

Multicolored polka-dot patterned

LAYOUT PAPER:

Lavender

SUPPLIES:

¼"-wide purple organdy ribbon

4¾"x2½" decorative label

Adhesive foam dots

Pinking shears

Protective keepsake box

Purple cardstock

Purple thread

Small square punch

Stickers: alphabet, dragonfly, flowers

Vellums: clear, embossed alphabet

DETAILS:

- (left) To create the keepsake pocket, cut the embossed alphabet vellum to approximately 4" shorter than the second page. Place the vellum piece on the page.

- Sew (3) sides of the vellum, leaving the top edge open.

- Punch a square in the center of the sides and bottom of the pocket, ¼" from the edges. For the top edge, punch through only the vellum and not the page.

- Thread a piece of ribbon through the top and bottom holes. Thread another piece through the side holes. Tie a knot in the ends of the ribbons in front of each hole.

- Secure the label, using an adhesive foam dot, in the center of pocket where the ribbons intersect.

First Day

BACKGROUND PAPER:

Green & pink striped

LAYOUT PAPER:

Pink toile patterned

SUPPLIES:

½"-wide green & pink hand-dyed silk ribbon

1¼" circular metal-edged vellum tag

Adhesive foam dots

Baby buggy die-cut

Green handmade paper

Mini silver brads

Stickers: alphabet, baby-themed

Yellow pastel chalk

DETAILS:

- (above right) For the title, tear a small strip from the handmade paper.

- Fold the paper with an accordion-style fold.

- Attach the strip, over a piece of ribbon, to the page with the brads.

- Spell out the word "MY" with the alphabet stickers on top of the strip.

- Continue with the stickers in spelling out "FIRST."

- Apply the "D" in the center of a tag. Secure the tag to the page, using an adhesive foam dot. Apply the rest of the stickers, in order, on the page.

Counting Sheep

BACKGROUND PAPER:

Dark pink textured cardstock

LAYOUT PAPER:

Multicolored striped

SUPPLIES:

Adhesive foam dots

Brads: mini silver, silver star

Clear vellum

Die-cuts: moon, sheep, premade title

Pink rickrack

Blake

BACKGROUND PAPER:

Blue cardstock

LAYOUT PAPERS:

Cloud patterned vellum

Yellow textured cardstock

SUPPLIES:

Alphabet stamps

Black ink pad

Eyelets: silver, teal ovals, blue square

Metal-edged paper tags

White thread

Word sticker

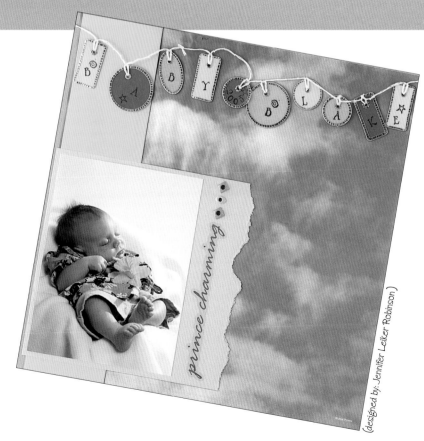

(designed by: Jennifer Leiker-Robinson)

Coming Home

BACKGROUND PAPER:

Green & purple floral striped

SUPPLIES:

¼"-wide purple sheer ribbon

½"-square wooden frame

3¾"x2¾" decorative paper frame

Adhesive foam dots

Clear vellum

Lavender acrylic paint

Medium paintbrush

Purple daisy photo corners

Purple mulberry paper

Small square punch

Wooden alphabet

DETAILS:

- Paint the wooden alphabet and frame with the lavender acrylic paint. Allow to dry completely.

- Arrange wooden alphabet to spell baby's name over large vellum journaling.

- Place the wooden frame in the center of the paper frame.

- Adhere each piece in place. Use an adhesive foam dot to secure a photo corner to the center in the wooden frame.

KAIRA

Comes home...

August 26th, 2003

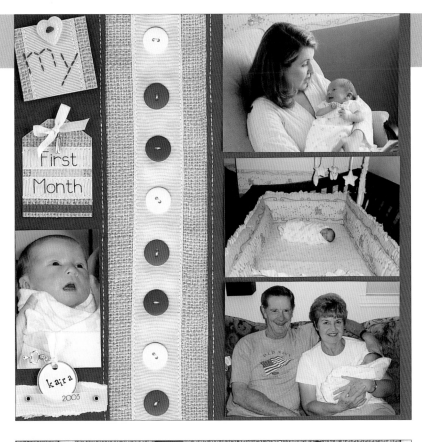

My First Month

BACKGROUND PAPER:

Button & textile patterned

LAYOUT PAPER:

Pink texture patterned

SUPPLIES:

1" circular metal-edged tags

Adhesive foam dots

Alphabet rubber stamps

Black ink pad

Charms: bottle, pacifier

Clear vellum

Cream heart-shaped button

Mini silver brads

Pink pastel chalk

Silk ribbons: ⅛"-wide maroon, ¼"-wide pink

Stitched alphabet stickers

Tag template

White fibers

DETAILS:

- (above left) To add the baby's name in the layout, stamp it onto a tag.
- Tear off a small piece from the pink texture patterned paper.
- Using an adhesive foam dot, center the tag on the paper.
- Place the journaled date over the tag and attach it to the page with brads.

First Smile

BACKGROUND PAPER:

Cream & pink floral patterned

LAYOUT PAPERS:

Texture patterned: dark pink, light pink

SUPPLIES:

¼"-wide pink variegated ribbon

Daisy punches: large, medium

Hole punches: medium, small

Pearl beads

Pink brad

Pink thread

Tag template

White artist paper

Handcrafted Cradle

BACKGROUND PAPER:

Pink cardstock

LAYOUT PAPER:

Green & pink patterned

SUPPLIES:

½"-wide pink hand-dyed silk ribbon

Adhesive foam dots

Baby-themed die-cuts

Clear vellum

Decorative frames: 3¾"-square, 4⅜"x4"

Nursery rhyme stickers

Pink lace doily

White thread

First Game

BACKGROUND PAPER:

Yellow cardstock

LAYOUT PAPER:

Yellow striped

SUPPLIES:

¼"-wide white organdy ribbon

Acetate

Adhesive foam tape

Alphabet template

Blue striped paper

Off-white cardstock

Square punches: large, medium

Silver eyelets and spiral paper clip

Small acrylic beads: blue, white

White thread

DETAILS:

- To create a shaker box, punch (2) large squares from the blue striped paper. Adhere one of the squares in place. Place a photograph on top of the square.

- Line the sides of the photograph with adhesive foam tape.

- Place the beads on top of the photograph, inside the tape perimeter.

- Punch out the interior of the second square to create a frame. Adhere acetate to the back side of the frame.

- Secure the second piece on top of the tape, trapping the beads inside.

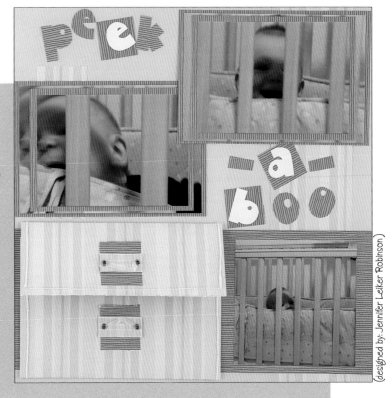

(designed by: Jennifer Leiker Robinson)

First Outing

BACKGROUND PAPER:

Yellow striped

LAYOUT PAPERS:

Floral patterned: dark pink, yellow

SUPPLIES:

⅝"-wide black gingham ribbon

1⅝"x2" brass frame

Adhesive foam dots

Clear vellum

Decorative-edged ruler

Key sticker

Mini silver brads

Punches: medium square, small circle

Yellow velvet flowers

First Photo Shoot

BACKGROUND PAPER:

Pink journal patterned

LAYOUT PAPER:

Pink striped

SUPPLIES:

1¼"-wide pink sinamay ribbon

Adhesive foam dots

Birth announcement

Heart sticker

Pink brads

White artist paper

Lexie

BACKGROUND PAPER:

Pink journal patterned

LAYOUT PAPER:

Pink cardstock

SUPPLIES:

Alphabet paper tags

Brown pastel chalk

Die-cuts: decorative tags, heart, ribbon

Twine

White artist paper

DETAILS:

- (above right) To create the title, mat one of the die-cuts on a torn piece of pink cardstock. Dust around the torn edge with the pastel chalk.

- Spell out the title with the paper tags. Thread the tags on a piece of twine and adhere them to the matted die-cut.

TIP For the matted photographs to stand out in the layout, choose a darker color of pastel chalk to add dimension from the background paper.

(designed by: The Scrapbook Haven)

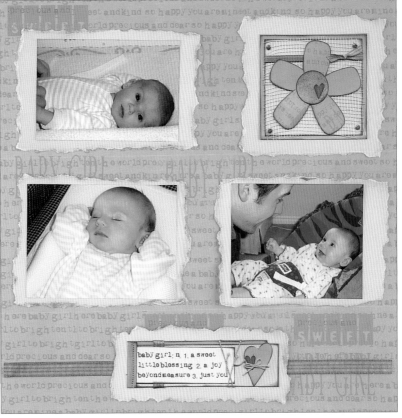

Sue's Blessing

BACKGROUND PAPER:

Green & pink striped

LAYOUT PAPER:

Cream floral patterned

SUPPLIES:

½"-wide light green organdy ribbon

2⅛"x1¼" floral nameplate

Adhesive foam dots

Alphabet stickers

Blessing certificate

Border template

Clear vellum envelope

Pinking shears

Small pearl beads

Vintage buttons

Mason's Blessing

BACKGROUND PAPER:

Baby blue cardstock

LAYOUT PAPER:

Blue toile patterned

SUPPLIES:

⅓"-square metal buckle

½"-wide light green organdy ribbon

2¾"x¾" metal nameplate

Adhesive foam dots

Clear vellum

Deckle-edged ruler

Heart-shaped nail heads

Large square template

Light blue paper flowers

Mini silver brads

Rub-on words

Kaira's Second Month

BACKGROUND PAPER:

Green

LAYOUT PAPER:

Multicolored striped

SUPPLIES:

Acrylic tokens

Dark pink paper

Mini silver brads

Off-white textured cardstock

Stickers: flower, word block

DETAILS:

- To coordinate the pages, cut strips from the striped paper. Adhere them, in a random pattern, vertically from the top edges of both pages.

- Apply the flower stickers to the ends of the color strips.

TIP Since the colors on these pages are so active, embellishments should be kept simple in order for the layout not to be overwhelming.

(designed by: The Scrapbook Haven)

First Bath in the Tub

BACKGROUND PAPER:

Orange & pink striped

LAYOUT PAPER:

Blue & pink polka-dot patterned

SUPPLIES:

Adhesive foam dots

Blue flower eyelets

Clear vellum

Duck die-cuts

Pink chenille rickrack

Pink thread

Temporary adhesive

Tiny baby. Big tub!

Kaira's first time in the big tub. –January 2004

DETAILS:

• Use a temporary adhesive to keep the photograph from moving before sewing the rickrack onto the page.

Yummy stuff!

Kaira had her first taste of Rice Cereal On December 26th, 2003. Delicious!

Yummy Stuff

BACKGROUND PAPER:

Orange & purple checkered

LAYOUT PAPERS:

Pink speckle patterned

Purple striped

SUPPLIES:

Adhesive foam dots

Baby-themed stickers

Pink rickrack

Purple eyelets

White artist paper

First Biscuit

BACKGROUND PAPER:

Multicolored striped

SUPPLIES:

⅜"-wide polka-dot satin ribbon

2¼" circular decorative tag

Adhesive foam dots

Alphabet rubber stamps

Alphabet stickers: large, small

Black ink pad

Blue square buttons

Clear vellum

Light green cardstock

Pink brads

Pink embroidery floss

Pink thread

DETAILS:

- To include the date in the layout, attach the journaled date to the tag with a brad.
- Thread the tag with a piece of ribbon and secure it to the page, using an adhesive foam dot.
- Finish labeling the date with a combination of the stamps and stickers.

First Halloween

BACKGROUND PAPER:
Purple speckle patterned

LAYOUT PAPER:
Orange striped

SUPPLIES:
1"-square metal-edged tag

26-gauge black plastic-covered wire

Adhesive foam dots

Black fibers

Craft knife

Eyelets: orange, purple

Halloween-themed die-cuts
(including bats, cat, moon,
trick-or-treat bag, and witch)

Mini silver brads

Small orange buttons

White artist paper

DETAILS:
- (above left) Attach each bat die-cut to the layout with purple eyelets.
- Thread a small piece of wire up through the eyelets and curl the excess wire ends.
- For the bat with the journaled date tag, attach the tag to the page with the wire and an orange eyelet.

First Time Carving Pumpkins

BACKGROUND PAPER:

Linen patterned

SUPPLIES:

Adhesive foam dots

Alphabet template

Alphabet tiles

Black journaling pen

Clear vellum

Mini orange eyelets

Orange fibers

Orange mulberry paper

Orange plaid patterned paper

Orange raffia

Pumpkin die-cuts

Red metallic thread

Tan cardstock

Yellow buttons

DETAILS:

- Using the template, spell out "PUMPKINS" on the orange plaid patterned paper.
- Cut out each letter and outline the edges with the journaling pen.
- Thread a piece of fiber through the cut-out letters—leaving enough space to the left of the letters for the vellum journaling.
- Tie the fiber ends through eyelets. Adhere each cut-out letter to the page.

First Thanksgiving

BACKGROUND PAPER:

Brown textured cardstock

LAYOUT PAPER:

Tan floral patterned

SUPPLIES:

3"-wide tan sinamay ribbon

Alphabet stickers

Brown pastel chalk

Mini silver brads

Silver buckle

White artist paper

KAIRA'S FIRST

THANKSGIVING

ON THANKSGIVING, WE WENT TO GRANDMA MARDEE'S FOR DINNER. KAIRA ENJOYED SEEING HER FAMILY, PLAYING "SUPER BABY" WITH DADDY, AND WATCHING THE FEAST! SHE WAS TOO LITTLE TO TRY ANY OF THE FOOD, BUT MOMMY'S TURKEY DINNER SEEMED TO MAKE KAIRA REALLY SLEEPY. SHE SLEPT THROUGH THE NIGHT FOR THE SECOND TIME!

-2003

DETAILS:

- (above) To add the journaling in the layout, print it on the artist paper. Crop the title from the rest of the journaling.

- With the alphabet stickers, spell out "BABY" on top of the title, and "THANKSGIVING" on top of the remaining journaling.

- Dust around the journaling with a small amount of the pastel chalk.

- Secure both the title and the journaling to the page with the brads.

First Snowstorm

BACKGROUND PAPER:

Off-white textured cardstock

LAYOUT PAPER:

Blue snowflake patterned

SUPPLIES:

1" circular metal-edged vellum tags

1¼"x1" silver mini frame

3"-wide blue sinamay ribbon

Clear vellum

Mini silver brads

Silver eyelets

Snowflake charms: large, small

White fibers

DETAILS:

- To accent the journaling, cut (2) pieces of the ribbon, large enough to go behind the title and the journaling vellum pieces.

- Using a small amount of clear adhesive, adhere the ribbon in place.

- Place the title and journaling over the ribbon and attach them to the page with the brads.

TIP Instead of using plain cardstock, try a textured cardstock. You'll add visual impact to your photographs and make your scrapbook pages look more professional.

First Christmas

BACKGROUND PAPER:

Green textured cardstock

LAYOUT PAPER:

Holly patterned

SUPPLIES:

5"x6⅓" decorative paper frame

Acid-free tape

Adhesive foam dots

Christmas card

Clear vellum

Die-cuts: button, gift, heart

Gold thread

Gold wire reindeer accent

Joy sticker

Mini gold brads

Red paper

Ribbons: ⅟₁₆"-wide gold-tasseled,
½"-wide gold metallic

DETAILS:

- (above right) Wrap (2) pieces of gold-tasseled ribbon around the top-left and bottom-right corners of the framed photograph. Secure them on the back of the cardstock with acid-free tape.

Kaira's first
Christmas

Kaira loved Christmas time! Kaira helped pick out a Christmas tree and decorated it with Mommy and Daddy. She would look at the lights and ornaments every day and, by Christmas, she was even reaching out to touch them. She enjoyed going to family Christmas parties and seeing her grandparents, aunt, uncles and cousins. She especially enjoyed meeting Santa Claus for the first time! On Christmas Eve, we made cookies and left them out for Santa. The next morning, the cookies were gone and Santa had left Kaira a stocking full of toys and a Together Tunes block. Kaira liked the block so much that she grabbed on to it and stood on her own for the very first time! Kaira loved all her new toys and had a wonderful First Christmas!

-2005-

Happy Holidays

May Your Holidays Be Merry and Bright!

With Love,
Tobin, Diana & Kaira

DETAILS:

- (below) To create the gift in the center of the page, wrap a piece of gold-tasseled ribbon on the gift die-cut. Secure the ribbon ends on the back side of the die-cut with acid-free tape.

- Create a bow from the metallic ribbon. Adhere a button die-cut to the center of the bow. Secure the bow to the gift die-cut, using an adhesive foam dot.

- Mat the gift die-cut onto a piece of red patterned paper and attach it the page with the brads.

- String the thread around the brads.

TIP Don't be afraid to change the look of an accent piece. This gift die-cut originally had a bow that didn't quite match the layout. I changed it to reflect the colors and feel of the layout.

DETAILS:

- (above) To accent a journaled section, tear a small piece from the journal and mount it to a piece of red paper.

- Attach the matted journaling to the page with the brads.

- String a piece of the gold-tasseled ribbon vertically across the journaling. Attach the ribbon in place by wrapping its ends around the brads.

TIP When you have many photographs of one event, consider a four-page layout. Use the same or similar accents to unify the layout.

First Valentines

BACKGROUND PAPER:

Pink striped

LAYOUT PAPERS:

Cardstocks: fuchsia,
light pink

SUPPLIES:

Clear vellum

Fuchsia buttons

Medium circle punch

Pink brads

Pink embroidery floss

Pink thread

Valentine cards

DETAILS:

- To create the layout, cut (3) rectangles from the fuchsia cardstock, making one large enough to be a pocket for the valentine cards.

- Using a straight stitch, sew all the fuchsia rectangles in place. (Refer to Stitches Guide on page 126.) For the pocket, leave the top edge open.

- Punch (18) circles from the light pink cardstock. Adhere the circles on the rectangles in a desired pattern.

Daddy's Valentine

BACKGROUND PAPER:

Pink gingham patterned

SUPPLIES:

½"-wide green hand-dyed silk ribbon

4"x2¾" decorative frame

Adhesive foam dots

Clear vellum

Mini silver brads

Pink paper

Stickers: floral, floral border, heart, quote

A Valentine love between Father and Daughter,
A love always precious and dear.
A daughter will always hold close to her heart,
where no other man could compare.

She may remain single, she may choose to wed,
but she will never belong to another.
No other eyes twinkle, no smiles quite the same,
as the beautiful face of her Father.

There's no one she trusts, so much in her life
the one who ate all her mud patties.
The one whose arms, always open and safe,
Her true love, her valentine....
DADDY!

DETAILS:

- To add the journaling in the layout, print it on the vellum. Cut both the journaling and a pink paper to 5"x9" pieces.
- Apply the ribbon to the top of the journaling, using an adhesive foam dot.
- Apply a sticker in front of the ribbon, securing it to the journaling.
- Attach the ribbon and the journaling to the page with brads.

Second Birthday

BACKGROUND PAPER:

Red cardstock

LAYOUT PAPER:

Purple flower patterned

SUPPLIES:

Circular punches: large, small

Clear vellum

Mini yellow brads

Yellow flower die-cuts

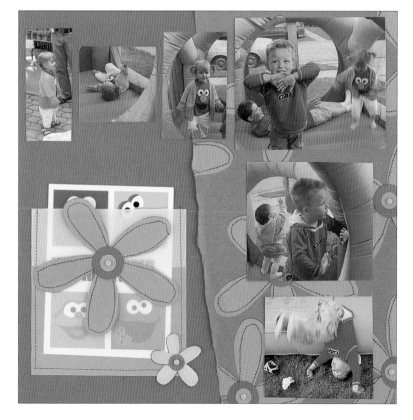

DETAILS:

- (left) To include the invitation in the layout, cut a piece from the vellum 1½" larger. Stitch the sides and bottom of vellum piece to the page.

- Punch a large circle from the cardstock and a small circle from the patterned paper. Layer them together.

- Crop a flower from the patterned paper and place it on top of the vellum pocket. Place the (2) circles in the center of the flower and secure the pieces to the vellum pocket with a brad.

TIP When cropping photographs, try not to crop things that will someday be of interest.

Colter's big boy
Bed

After Colter jumped out of his crib for the 5th time, we decided it was time for a big boy bed. We found this great "car" bed and hoped Colter would actually sleep in it! After a few nights of lying with him as he fell asleep, he was fine. He loved this bed!
—March 1996

Big Boy Bed

BACKGROUND PAPER:
Yellow speckle patterned

LAYOUT PAPER:
Blue star patterned

SUPPLIES:
28-gauge silver wire
Brads: red, silver star
Large moon-shaped punch
Star die-cuts
White vellum

DETAILS:
• Attach the die-cuts to the journaling with the wire and silver star brads.

First Day of School

BACKGROUND PAPER:
Multicolored block patterned

SUPPLIES:
Adhesive foam dots
Clear vellum
Flower stickers
Pink plastic rivets

DETAILS:
• To add the journaling on the page, print it on the vellum. Attach the journaling on the page with rivets, placing the rivets along the left-hand side of the journaling.

Justine's first day of school!
Justine set off to Kindergarten with her "Meg" backpack. She liked her teacher, Mrs. Price, but her favorite thing about school? The monkey bars of course!
—September 1997

First Day of Kindergarten

BACKGROUND PAPER:

White cardstock

LAYOUT PAPERS:

Black cardstock

Patterned: blue plaid, school bus

Red

Red striped

SUPPLIES:

Alphabet template

Jesse

BACKGROUND PAPER:

Kraft cardstock

LAYOUT PAPERS:

Green cardstock

Swirl patterned papers: navy blue, green

SUPPLIES:

⅓"x¼" silver conchas

Alphabet rubber stamps

Alphabet stickers

Clear photo corners

Clear vellum

Large silver star eyelets

Navy blue cardstock and fibers

Purple ink pad

(designed by: Sherri Wright)

Colter's First Ride

BACKGROUND PAPERS:

Cardstocks: blue, gray

SUPPLIES:

22-gauge dark pink
plastic-covered wire

Adhesive foam dots

Alphabet template

Black journaling pen

Black thread

Boy with bicycle die-cut

Paper crimper

Red cardstock

Small square punch

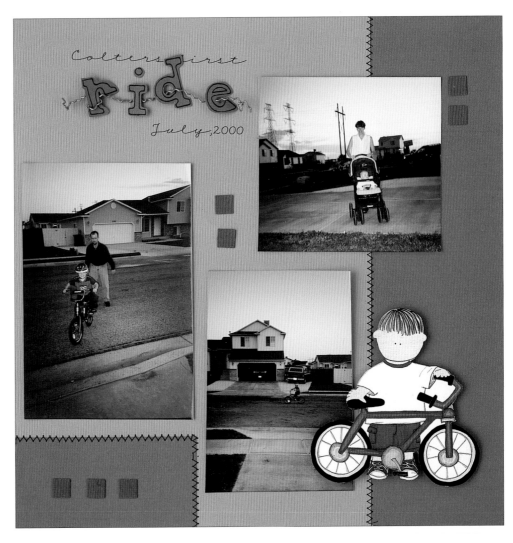

DETAILS:

- To create the background for the scrapbook page, cut an 8½"x12" piece from the gray cardstock. Print the journaling onto the gray cardstock piece.

- Cut a 3½"x12" piece and a 4¼"x2" piece from the blue cardstock.

- Using a zigzag stitch, sew the larger piece to the right side of the gray cardstock and the smaller piece to the bottom-left corner of the gray cardstock. (Refer to Stitches Guide on page 126.)

Fourth Birthday

BACKGROUND PAPER:

Green block patterned

SUPPLIES:

Clear vellum

Event memorabilia

Green eyelets

Stickers: polka dot, star

DETAILS:

- To add the journaling to the layout, print it on the vellum.
- Cut the journaling into (2) pieces. Attach both journaling pieces to the pages with the eyelets.
- To create the memorabilia pocket, attach an eyelet at the bottom of a piece of journaling.
- Place the event memorabilia behind the journaling.

TIP To save space, make a pocket (for cards) out of part of the journaling. This way, you have more room for the photographs and still can include the cards.

Fifth Birthday

BACKGROUND PAPER:

Light blue textured cardstock

LAYOUT PAPERS:

Dark blue textured cardstock

Green speckle patterned

SUPPLIES:

Adhesive foam dots

Birthday-themed die-cuts

Buttons: blue, yellow

Clear vellum

Light green brads

Light green embroidery floss

Stickers: alphabet, words

DETAILS:

- (above right) To create the journaling, print it on the vellum. Separate the title. Attach both journaling pieces to the first page with the brads.

- Finish the title with the alphabet stickers. Secure the stickers to the page, using adhesive foam dots.

TIP Use embellishments like eyelets, buttons, or brads to make your die-cuts look more unique. You could even hand-stitch around them with embroidery floss, or accent them with wire. The possibilities are endless to create a one-of-a-kind look from a premade product.

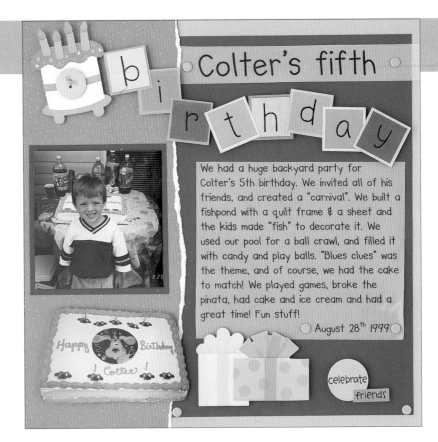

Colter's fifth birthday

We had a huge backyard party for Colter's 5th birthday. We invited all of his friends, and created a "carnival". We built a fishpond with a quilt frame & a sheet and the kids made "fish" to decorate it. We used our pool for a ball crawl, and filled it with candy and play balls. "Blues clues" was the theme, and of course, we had the cake to match! We played games, broke the pinata, had cake and ice cream and had a great time! Fun stuff!

August 28th 1999

celebrate friends

Grandpa Clark

BACKGROUND PAPER:

Navy blue cardstock

LAYOUT PAPER:

Plaid patterned vellum

SUPPLIES:

¼"-wide green organdy ribbon

Cardstocks: kraft, white

Clear vellum

Eyelets: alphabet, words

Fern leaf charm plaque

Green handmade paper

Navy blue snaps

Personalized journaling

Rub-on word

Silver eyelets

(designed by: Sariah Wilson)

DETAILS:

- To make the journaling pocket, cut a 6½"x4½" piece from the kraft cardstock.
- To make the accordion folds for the cardstock piece, fold in the sides 1", then again approximately ½" in.
- Cut a 3½"x4½" piece from the plaid vellum. Place the vellum piece on the front of the kraft pocket, under the second fold.
- Place a photograph on top of the vellum piece. Attach both to the kraft piece with the eyelets.
- Line the back of the kraft piece with handmade paper.
- Adhere the finished pocket to the page.

A Mother

BACKGROUND PAPER:

Embossed button patterned

LAYOUT PAPER:

Copper embossed journal patterned

SUPPLIES:

1⅜"-wide copper sheer ribbon

2" oval copper frame

Acid-free tape

Copper brads

Cream embossed floral patterned paper

Heart charm

A Mother holds her Childs hand for a little while, their hearts forever....
I think this quote is perfect for this photograph. I love the tenderness between my dad and my grandmother. We may no longer need to hold their hands, but mothers *always* hold us in their hearts.

-1948

DETAILS:

- To attach the ribbon on the page, punch (2) squares directly above the journaling. Thread the ribbon through the first square and out the second. Thread the small tail end back through the first hole.

- Take the long end of the ribbon and repeat on the second hole.

- Cut the ends of the ribbon in a "V" shape.

- To place the frame on the page, loop ribbon on both sides of the frame. Secure the ribbon ends on the back side of the page, using acid-free tape.

Family Legacy

BACKGROUND PAPER:

Kraft cardstock

LAYOUT PAPER:

Tan cardstock

SUPPLIES:

Black journaling pen

Brown cardstock

Brown pastel chalks

Square punches: large, medium

Tag template

Tan eyelets

Word definition patterned paper

DETAILS:

- Crumple the patterned paper and lightly dust it with the pastel chalk.

Dad, Mom, Noah @ 6 wks, W.F., Texas by

(designed by: Jennifer Leiker Robinson)

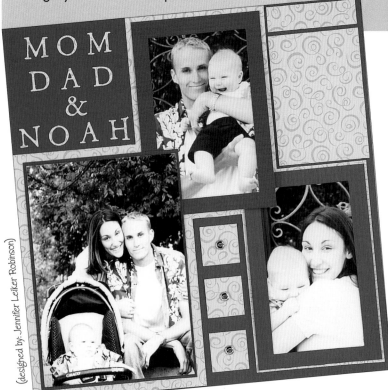

(designed by: Jennifer Leiker Robinson)

Mom, Dad & Noah

BACKGROUND PAPER:

Navy blue textured cardstock

LAYOUT PAPER:

Gray patterned

SUPPLIES:

Button nail heads

Craft knife

Punches: alphabet, medium square

Our Family

BACKGROUND PAPER:

Green cardstock

LAYOUT PAPERS:

Cardstocks:
blue, kraft

SUPPLIES:

Alphabet templates

Black cardstock

Black embroidery
floss

Black journaling
pen

Brown pastel
chalk

Craft knife

Quote die-cut label

(designed by: Jennifer Leiker Robinson)

DETAILS:

- To create the title, trace and cut "OUR" and "2003" from the black cardstock, and "FAMILY" from the kraft cardstock.

- Trace around the kraft cardstock letters with the journaling pen.

- Overlap "OUR" with "FAMILY."

- Adhere each letter in place.

TIP To create a harmonious feel for your layout, limit your color use to only the hues found in the photo.

Little Things

BACKGROUND PAPER:

Red speckle patterned

LAYOUT PAPER:

Green cardstock

SUPPLIES:

Brass eyelets

Brown pastel chalk

Cardstocks: tan, white

Clear vellum

Jute

Small circle punch

Enjoy the *little things* in life for **one day** you may **look back** and *realize* they were the **Big things**

Ethan   2003   Allie Jo

(designed by: Lesha Dalebout)

DETAILS:

- To accent the journaling, carefully tear small sections from the tan cardstock to highlight selected words. Dust around the torn edges of the cardstock sections with the pastel chalk. Adhere them to the green cardstock piece.

- Attach the journaling in place with the eyelets.

- To create the journaled tag, place the journaled names and date onto pieces of white cardstock.

- Cut out tag shapes from both the journaled vellum and the cardstock. Punch a hole near the top edge of the tags. Tear the bottom edge of the tags.

Love

BACKGROUND PAPER:

Celery cardstock

LAYOUT PAPER:

Heart patterned

SUPPLIES:

¼"-wide pink feather-edged ribbon

Cardstocks: pink textured, sunflower

Silver eyelets

Small circle punch

Templates: alphabet, large tag

(designed by: Kimber Stoddard)

DETAILS:

- To create the title, trace and cut out the letters from the sunflower cardstock. Mat each letter on celery cardstock. Attach an eyelet in the center of the "O" and the "E."

- Using the tag template, make (4) tags from the pink textured cardstock. Place a piece of heart patterned paper near the top of the tag and punch a hole through both pieces of paper.

- Loop pieces of ribbon through each hole.

- Adhere each matted letter to a tag.

- Tear (4) pieces of celery cardstock and adhere them to each tag, under the letters.

- Adhere the tags in place.

(designed by: Breanna Berntsen for Memory Lane Paper Co.)

BACKGROUND PAPER:

Pink journal patterned

LAYOUT PAPER:

Dark pink cardstock

SUPPLIES:

¼"- wide pink variegated ribbon

Acid-free tape

Cardstocks: light pink, lavender

Clear vellum

Dark pink brads

Eyelet word

Metal photo corners

Plastic word pebble

Silver metal word charms

DETAILS:

- To accent the page, cut a 9¼"x5¾" piece from the dark and light pink cardstocks.

- Cut an 8"x5⅓" piece from the purple cardstock. Wrap a piece of ribbon twice around the top of the dark pink piece. Secure the ribbon on the back side with acid-free tape.

- Adhere the dark pink piece vertically on the page, approximately 1"from the top-left corner.

- Attach the photo corners to the bottom corners of the adhered piece.

- Crumple the edges of the light pink piece and secure the lavender piece in the center.

My Aunt

BACKGROUND PAPER:

Purple cardstock

SUPPLIES:

Adhesive foam dots

Cardstocks: cream, green

Green colored pencil

Heart template

Mini heart punch

Pebble word

Small heart punch

White fiber

I'm so glad you're my aunt

Claire just adores all her aunts. Anytime she sees one, her face totally lights up. Rebecca loves to spoil Claire. These photos were taken during Maggie's graduation celebration. It captures their relationship so well, these are some of my favorite pictures.

(designed by: Liz Taylor)

DETAILS:
- To create the title, print the journaling on the cream cardstock.
- Cut out each word for the title. Cut out "AUNT" using the template.
- Mat the journaling pieces onto green and purple cardstocks.
- Using the heart punch, punch a few hearts to accent the matted "AUNT."
- Color the journaled word "MY" with the green colored pencil.
- Adhere each matted word, in order, on the page.
- To add interest, secure every other word of the title, using an adhesive foam dot.

Cousins

BACKGROUND PAPER:

Navy blue textured cardstock

LAYOUT PAPERS:

Cardstocks: red, white

SUPPLIES:

¼"-wide white organdy ribbon

Adhesive foam dots

Alphabet template

Punches: large square, small square

White embroidery floss

White eyelets

White journaling pen

(designed by: Jennifer Leiker Robinson)

DETAILS:

- To create the title, punch (7) large squares from the red cardstock and (3) large squares from the blue cardstock.

- Using the template, trace the letters and numbers on the squares. Pierce holes all around the traced letters and numbers. Stitch each hole with the embroidery floss.

- Punch (7) small squares from the navy cardstock and (3) from the red cardstock. Place the small squares onto the large squares, in the center of the left-hand side. Attach the pieces together with an eyelet.

- Attach each square to the page, using an adhesive foam dot.

- Thread the ribbon through the eyelets, tying the ends in the front.

The Best

BACKGROUND PAPER:

Green

LAYOUT PAPER:

Cream floral patterned

SUPPLIES:

Clear vellum   Purple cardstock

Green paper   Silver flower eyelets

DETAILS:

- As an alternative to cropping the photograph, place a piece of vellum over it. Then carefully tear out the center of the vellum to expose the photograph beneath.

(designed by: Lesha Dalebout)

Backyard Buddies

BACKGROUND PAPER:

Blue checkered

LAYOUT PAPER:

Red cardstock

SUPPLIES:

Alphabet die-cuts   Large square punch

Blue eyelets   White cardstock

DETAILS:

- To create visual interest near the bottom of the page, crop the photographs to the same size by using the large square punch.

(designed by: Lesha Dalebout)

Suzanne & Missy

BACKGROUND PAPER:

Green & blue plaid patterned

SUPPLIES:

Adhesive foam dots

Blue mulberry paper

Clear vellum

Gold fibers and star charms

Mini gold brads

Scrap of red cardstock

Stickers: bicycle, flag, fruit border, pie, word banner

DETAILS:

- For the flag sticker, place the sticker on a scrap piece of red cardstock. Trim off the excess cardstock.

Aunt Mardee

BACKGROUND PAPER:

Floral striped

LAYOUT PAPER:

Butterfly patterned

SUPPLIES:

¼"-wide dark pink silk ribbon

3½"x5" decorative frame

Adhesive foam dots

Butterfly stickers

Clear vellum

Cream mulberry paper

Light blue rickrack

Multicolored striped paper

My Very Best Friend

BACKGROUND PAPER:

Black cardstock

LAYOUT PAPER:

Pink polka-dot patterned

SUPPLIES:

1⅞"-wide metal-edged pink vellum tags

Acid-free tape

Large circle punch

Pink slide mount

Pink tulle

Silver flower brads

White cardstock

(designed by: Kimber Stoddard for Memory Lane Paper Co.)

DETAILS:

- For the bottom tags, print the journaling on the white cardstock.
- Punch each journaled section out and place them under the tags.
- Attach the tags and the journaling to the page with the brads.

Roscoe

BACKGROUND PAPERS:

Multicolored block patterned

Multicolored striped

SUPPLIES:

½"-wide green silk ribbon

Acid-free tape

Adhesive foam dots

Alphabet stickers

Decorative paper tags

Doghouse charm

Green cardstock

Silver chain

Square alphabet beads

DETAILS:

- On one of the tags, spell out the word "PUPPY" with the stickers.

- Tie a charm onto the ribbon.

- Secure the tag to the first page, using an adhesive foam dot.

- String the beads onto the chain to spell out the puppy's name.

- Drape the chain over the top of a tag. Secure the chain to the back of the tag with acid-free tape.

- Secure the tag to the second page with an adhesive foam dot.

BACKGROUND PAPER:
Red cardstock

LAYOUT PAPERS:
Black handmade
Compass patterned acetate

SUPPLIES:
1"-square metal buckle
1 ½"-wide black gingham ribbon
Acid-free tape
Black fibers
Clear vellum
Mini silver brads
Vintage image

DETAILS:
- To accent the left-hand side of the page, place the acetate over the background paper. Adhere it in place on the left-hand side of the page.
- Tear a 3½"x12" piece from the handmade paper. Adhere it in place on the left-hand side of the page.
- Thread the buckle on a piece of ribbon. Drape the ribbon over the top-left corner of the page. Secure the ribbon ends on the back side with acid-free tape.

TIP Download the vintage image from the Internet, resize it, and place on the layout.

Wedding 1912

BACKGROUND PAPER:

Blue floral patterned

SUPPLIES:

Mini silver brads

Original handwritten letter

Purple mulberry paper

Stickers: floral borders, word

Vellums: clear, tan journal patterned

Velvet flowers: cream, purple

White thread

Thomas Wilford England
Bertha Rebecca Robson England
April 3, 1912

DETAILS:

- To secure the handwritten letter to the page, tear a strip from the mulberry paper as wide as the folded letter.

- Apply a word sticker on top of the strip.

- Place a cream velvet flower on the right-hand side of the word sticker.

- Attach the strip and velvet flower to the page, using the brads.

- Tuck the letter behind the strip.

TIP If you are concerned about the acid content of your precious photographs, make copies and have them printed on acid-free paper.

Grandma & Grandpa England's Wedding

BACKGROUND PAPER:

Tan floral patterned

SUPPLIES:

½"-wide pink silk ribbon

3½"x1" decorative label

5⅞"x7⅞" floral frame

Adhesive foam dots

Clear vellum

Heart necklace & earring set

Hydrangea garland

Mini gold brads

Pink embroidery floss

Stickers: floral border, small floral

DETAILS:

- To create a floral frame for a 5"x7" photograph, cut (2) 8" strips and (2) 6" strips from the patterned paper. Cut the 6" strips diagonally at each end (one end with a diagonal cut going up, one end with a diagonal cut going down). Adhere all pieces together.

- Mount the photographs in the center of the frame and adhere the frame in place.

TIP Dollar stores are a great place to find charms, jewelry, and other fun things for your pages. On this page, the posts were removed from the earrings and the chain from the necklace to make heart charms. You could do the same with just about any jewelry piece.

Mom &
Dad's Wedding

BACKGROUND PAPER:

Light green floral patterned

SUPPLIES:

½"-wide light green silk ribbon

Mauve mesh

Pewter stickers

Pink textured cardstock

Pink velvet flowers

Vintage cards

Wedding announcement

White gem buttons

White thread

DETAILS:

• To make a French bulletin board, place the ribbon on the page at a diagonal, approximately 2" apart. Adhere the ribbon ends on the back side with acid-free tape.

• Do the same on the opposite diagonal.

• Adhere the buttons where the ribbons intersect.

• Place the cards and announcement on the page, placing some of the corners under the ribbon.

BACKGROUND PAPER:

Multicolored striped

LAYOUT PAPER:

Blue cardstock

SUPPLIES:

2½"-square blue plastic frame

2½"-wide maroon toile-printed ribbon

Acid-free tape

Adhesive foam dots

Alphabet eyelets

Alphabet stickers

Clear vellum

Rub-on words

Travel-themed die-cuts

White thread

TIP Mini frames are a great embellishment for a scrapbook page. They need not have anything in them to make a great page accent. Simply thread ribbon through one to make a decorative "buckle."

DETAILS:

- Place the journaling in the center of the frame. Tie the ribbon onto the frame and drape the ribbon end over the top edge of the page.

- Stitch the ribbon's knot onto the page. Secure the ribbon on the back side of the page, using acid-free tape.

(designed by: Sherri Wright)

Cherish

BACKGROUND PAPER:

Cream journal patterned

LAYOUT PAPER:

Romantic text patterned acetate

SUPPLIES:

Acid-free tape

Eyelet word

Green cardstock

Key charms

White tasseled fibers

DETAILS:

• To secure acetate to page, attach an eyelet word to page bottom and thread the fiber around top of page.

Husband & Wife

BACKGROUND PAPER:

Cream cardstock

LAYOUT PAPERS:

Cardstocks: light gray, off-white

SUPPLIES:

¼"-wide white feather-edged ribbon

Eyelet words

Heart paper clips

Mini silver brads

Rub-on alphabet

Translucent photo corners

(designed by: Sherri Wright)

Now & Forever

BACKGROUND PAPER:

Black & white journal patterned

LAYOUT PAPER:

Black cardstock

SUPPLIES:

Alphabet stickers

Clear photo corners

Clear vellum

Mini silver brads

Necklace with circle charm

Rub-on words

Templates:
medium rectangle,
medium square,
small circle

White cardstock

White mulberry paper

(designed by: Sherri Wright)

DETAILS:

• To create small window frames, trace and cut rectangular and square holes down the left-hand side of the black cardstock. Adhere the cardstock over the patterned paper.

• To personalize the charm, trace and cut a small circle from the patterned paper. Adhere the circle to the charm and secure the necklace to the back side of the page.

Eternal Love

BACKGROUND PAPERS:

Cardstocks: red, white

LAYOUT PAPERS:

Cardstocks: red, white

SUPPLIES:

2⅓"-square decorative metal frame

Acid-free tape

Alphabet tiles

Heart paper clip

Mini silver brads

Red heart patterned paper

Rub-on words

White fibers

White mulberry paper

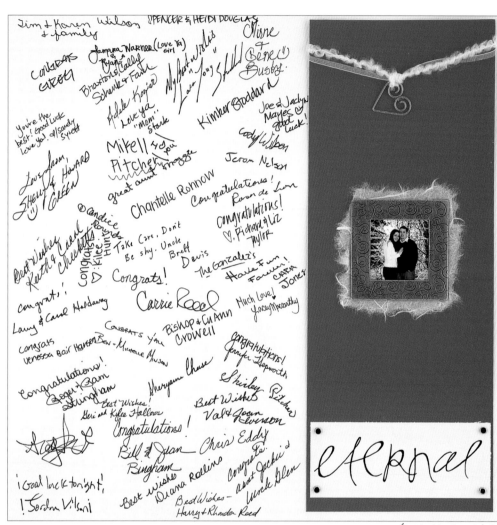

(designed by: Sherri Wright)

DETAILS:

• To accent the right-hand side of the page, cut a 4½"x11⅓" strip from the red cardstock.

• Thread a piece of white fiber at the top of the red strip.

• Secure the fiber ends to the back side of the strip with acid-free tape.

• Attach the clip in the center of the fiber.

• Adhere the entire red strip to the page.

TIP The artist created this layout for her guests to sign at her wedding. This way, she'll always have a written account of what feelings her guests had on her special day.

DETAILS:

- To double mat the photograph, place it onto a piece of white cardstock and a piece of patterned paper. Adhere the matted photograph to the top-left corner of the page.

- To add the journaling, cut a 5⅓"x2½" strip from the white cardstock. Apply a rub-on word to the white strip. Attach the strip in place with the brads.

DETAILS:

- To add the couple's information to the layout, spell out each name and the date of the wedding, using the tiles. Adhere each tile in place.

Happiness

BACKGROUND PAPER:

Off-white cardstock

SUPPLIES:

⅓"-wide cream printed twill ribbon

2"-square metal-edged vellum tag

Acid-free tape

Black cardstock

Black fiber

Rub-on word

Washer word

DETAILS:

- Remove the center of the tag. Place a small photograph inside of the tag and secure it on a piece of black cardstock.

(designed by: Sherri Wright)

Honor, Love & Cherish

BACKGROUND PAPER:

Green floral patterned

LAYOUT PAPER:

Green floral embossed vellum

SUPPLIES:

⅜"-square metal buckle

Adhesive foam dots

Mini silver brads

Ribbons: ¼"-wide green fancy woven, ½"-wide green organdy

Stickers: alphabet, white silk flowers

White rub-on words

Wedding Love

BACKGROUND PAPER:

Green embossed floral patterned cardstock

LAYOUT PAPERS:

Green floral patterned

Green striped

SUPPLIES:

⅝"-wide green organdy ribbon

Border template

Green fibers

Heart sticker

Small circle punch

DETAILS:

- To coordinate the pages, trace and cut (2) borders from the patterned paper with the template. Attach each border to a page.
- Cut (2) strips from of the striped paper, and adhere them to the centers of the borders.

TIP When attaching many photographs to a layout, try not to overwhelm the page with page accents. Keep it simple! Let the photographs speak for themselves.

Hill Wedding

BACKGROUND PAPER:

Cream & green striped

LAYOUT PAPERS:

Green embossed floral patterned vellum

Green floral patterned paper

SUPPLIES:

⅝"-wide green organdy ribbon

Adhesive foam dots

Border template

Green fibers

Rub-on words

Silver mini brads

Stickers: pewter, white silk flowers, word definition

Wedding memorabilia

White cardstock

DETAILS:

- To document the event, use the wedding memorabilia as page accents.
- Layer the memorabilia together and accent them with stickers, fibers, and brads.

TIP To preserve the information on the invitation, ceremony card, and napkin, scan and print the items onto white cardstock.

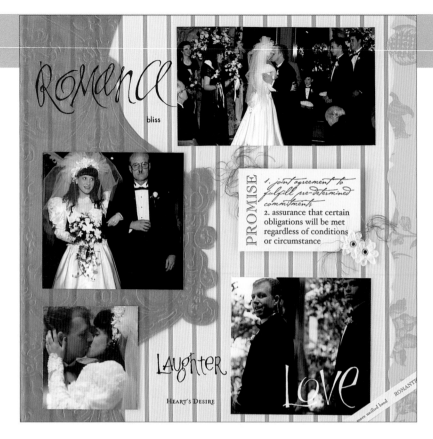

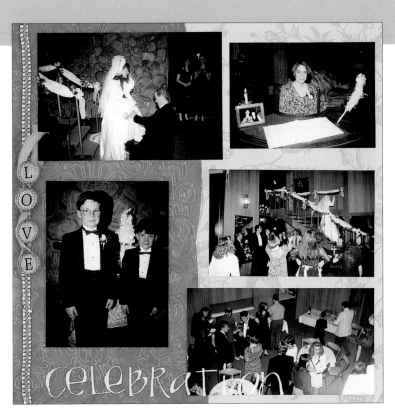

Wedding Celebration

BACKGROUND PAPER:

Green floral patterned

LAYOUT PAPER:

Green embossed floral patterned vellum

SUPPLIES:

Adhesive foam dots

Alphabet stickers

Ribbons: ¼"-wide green fancy woven, ½"-wide green hand-dyed silk

Rub-on words

DETAILS:

- To create the page borders, tear the vellum in half. Adhere a half to each page.

- Using a straight stitch, sew the fancy woven ribbon onto the page edges. (Refer to Stitches Guide on page 126.)

- Secure the stickers over the sewn ribbon, using adhesive foam dots.

- Thread pieces of silk ribbon around each sticker.

Our Tenth Anniversary

BACKGROUND PAPER:
Green embossed cardstock

LAYOUT PAPER:
Cream floral patterned

SUPPLIES:
4"x¾" copper tag
4⅛"x9½" cream envelope
Acid-free tape
Adhesive foam dots
Clear vellum
Copper brads
Copper heart charm
Dimensional photo corners
Dimensional stickers: nameplate, watch face
Embossed vellum die-cuts
Event memorabilia
Fibers: cream-tasseled, tan

DETAILS:
- (above right) Thread the charm onto a piece of cream-tasseled fiber.
- Wrap the fiber horizontally near the top edge of the first page. Secure the ends on the back side with acid-free tape.
- Secure the charm on the journaling, using an adhesive foam dot.

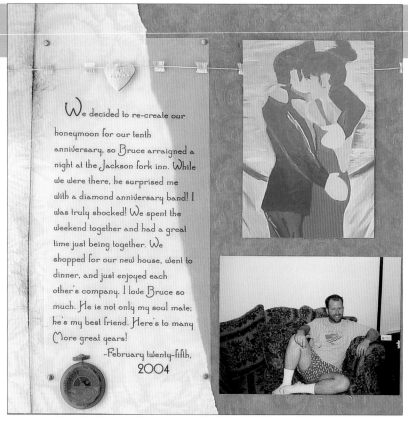

We decided to re-create our honeymoon for our tenth anniversary, so Bruce arraigned a night at the Jackson fork inn. While we were there, he surprised me with a diamond anniversary band! I was truly shocked! We spent the weekend together and had a great time just being together. We shopped for our new house, went to dinner, and just enjoyed each other's company. I love Bruce so much. He is not only my soul mate; he's my best friend. Here's to many more great years!

-February twenty-fifth, 2004

Girl's Night

BACKGROUND PAPER:

Multicolored block

SUPPLIES:

Alphabet rubber stamp

Alphabet stickers

Black ink pad

Brass rivets

Brown cardstock

Circular die-cuts: large, medium

Clear vellum

White vellum

DETAILS:

- Use the large circular die-cuts for the page title.
- Spell out the page title by combining the alphabet stamps and stickers.
- Place the matted title on top of the journaling panel to cover up the adhesive mark.

TIP Be careful in choosing your font style and placement since both will effect the mood of the layout.

Freedom

BACKGROUND PAPER:

Tan speckle patterned

LAYOUT PAPER:

Patterned: brown speckle, flag

SUPPLIES:

24-gauge silver wire

Alphabet stickers

Black cardstock

Brown pastel chalk

Clear vellum

Craft knife

Jute

Military dog tags

Patriotic-themed stickers

Rub-on alphabet

Tag template

(designed by: The Scrapbook Haven)

DETAILS:

- (above) To create a frame for the photograph, tear out a 7½" square from the center of the flag patterned paper. Adhere the frame to the first page. Adhere the torn-out piece near the top-left corner of the second page.

- To create the tag on the first page, trace and cut a tag from the tan speckle patterned paper. Adhere scraps from the brown speckle patterned paper to the tag. Dust the edges of the scraps and tags with the pastel chalk. Thread the tag with a piece of jute.

- Apply the "COURAGE" sticker to a piece of black cardstock and adhere a piece of vellum over the sticker. Adhere the piece to the center of the tag. Adhere the tag in the top-left corner of the frame.

A Hero's Welcome

BACKGROUND PAPER:
Tan textured cardstock

LAYOUT PAPER:
World map patterned

SUPPLIES:
⅜"-square metal buckles

⅜"-wide brown word ribbon

¾"x1½" metal-edged vellum tags

1½"-square decorative copper frame

Adhesive foam dots

Alphabet rubber stamps

Black ink pad

Clear vellum

Cream linen thread

Die-cuts: alphabet, patriotic-themed

Event memorabilia

Eyelets: silver, silver alphabet

Mini copper brads

Mustard cardstock

Stickers: alphabet, button

In February of 2003, Braden left for a tour of duty in Iraq. We were all so worried about him. Finally, more than a year later, we received word he would be coming home! On the day he was to arrive, the boys made posters, grabbed there flags, and we headed to the airport. His flight came in early, so we couldn't greet him as he got off the plane, but we were still able to give him a hero's welcome. Later, we drove to Wade and Jo's for a welcome home party. As we drove to the house, we were amazed! There were flags & banners lining the street all the way to the house! It was beautiful! Their house was absolutely covered in yellow ribbons and flags. There were tons of neighbors, family and friends. Even the news media attended. Brandt played a patriotic song on the bagpipes (he is so talented), and we all enjoyed visiting with our family, especially Braden. He has matured so much, and we are so proud of him! He is defiantly a hero in our eyes!

● March 29th 2004 ●

DETAILS:

- (above right) To accent the main photograph, mat it onto a piece of mustard cardstock. Attach the matted photograph to the page with the brads.

- Wrap a piece of thread between the top (2) brads.

- Stamp the word "PRIDE" on a tag. Attach the tag to the thread, tying a knot in the front.

- Wrap another piece of thread between the bottom (2) brads, tying the knot off-center. Apply a button sticker to the center of the knot.

Olympic-sized Excitement

BACKGROUND PAPER:

Black textured cardstock

LAYOUT PAPER:

Red-orange textured cardstock

SUPPLIES:

Adhesive foam dots

Alphabet template

Black journaling pen

Blue brads

Blue fibers

Blue triangular patterned paper

Clear vellum

Die-cuts: circular alphabet, Olympic-themed

Eyelets: alphabet, silver

Orange artist paper

Yellow textured cardstock

DETAILS:

- To include the date and location on the layout, cut (2) scraps from the yellow cardstock. Adhere one to the first page.

- For the scrap on the second page, attach with silver eyelets.

- Alternating the alphabet die-cuts and the alphabet eyelets, spell out the location and year of the event. Attach each word on top of a yellow scrap.

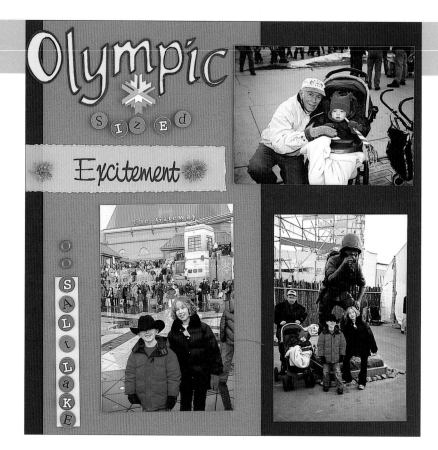

Benton
Family Reunion

BACKGROUND PAPER:

Green textured cardstock

LAYOUT PAPER:

Strawberry patterned

SUPPLIES:

3"-wide cream sinamay ribbon

Butterfly die-cut

Clear vellum

Craft knife

Mini silver brads

Red plaid patterned paper

DETAILS:

- (above right) To accent the title, tear the strawberry patterned paper in half. Adhere one half to the left-hand side of the first page.

- Cut a 12" piece of ribbon to 2¼" wide. Place it vertically over the patterned paper on the first page.

- Cut a 4¾"x1¾" strip from the plaid patterned paper and adhere it behind the ribbon, near the top-left corner of the first page.

- Place the title over the strip. Attach a die-cut to the top-right corner of the title with a brad. Attach the bottom-left corner of the title to the page with a brad.

- Using the craft knife, cut out images from the strawberry patterned paper. Adhere one of the images over the top-left corner of the title.

Suzanne's Graduation

BACKGROUND PAPER:

Tan textured cardstock

LAYOUT PAPER:

Inspirational text patterned acetate

SUPPLIES:

½"-wide green hand-dyed silk ribbon

1"-square metal buckle

Cream cardstock

Event memorabilia

Green fibers

Metal photo corners

Mini silver brads

Texture patterned papers: burnt sienna, green

Graduation

BACKGROUND PAPER:

Navy blue cardstock

LAYOUT PAPER:

Yellow cardstock

SUPPLIES:

Adhesive foam dot

Clear vellum

Graduation hat die-cut

Graduation invitation

Rub-on words

White cardstock

(designed by: Sherri Wright)

Colter's Citizen of the Year Award

BACKGROUND PAPER:

Red cardstock

LAYOUT PAPER:

Blue cardstock

SUPPLIES:

Blue brads

Blue embroidery floss

Clear vellum

Yellow buttons

Yellow cardstock

DETAILS:

- Adhere a piece of cardstock behind the journaling.

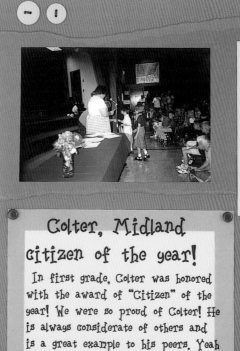

Colter, Midland citizen of the year!

In first grade, Colter was honored with the award of "Citizen" of the year! We were so proud of Colter! He is always considerate of others and is a great example to his peers. Yeah Colt!

—May 31st, 2001

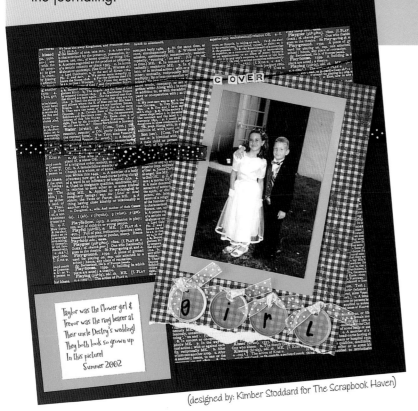

Taylor was the flower girl & Trevor was the ring bearer at their uncle Destry's wedding! They both look so grown up in this picture!
Summer 2002

(designed by: Kimber Stoddard for The Scrapbook Haven)

Cover Girl

BACKGROUND PAPER:

Black textured cardstock

LAYOUT PAPER:

Black & white journal patterned

SUPPLIES:

⅜"-wide polka-dot ribbons: black, pink

1 ¼" circular metal-edged pink vellum tags

Alphabet beads

Black & pink checkered paper

Black journaling pen

Black string

Cardstocks: pink, white

Mom's Birthday

BACKGROUND PAPER:

Sage green floral patterned

SUPPLIES:

¼"-wide purple sheer ribbon

Adhesive foam dots

Alphabet stickers

Cardstocks: multicolored block patterned, purple

Clear vellum

Multicolored striped paper

Teal green swirl patterned paper

Punches: large square, medium rectangle, small circle

Purple daisy photo corners

Silver spiral paper clip

Tags: 2" circular metal-edged vellum, 2¼"-square decorative paper

Atholeen's Birthday

BACKGROUND PAPER:

Green gingham patterned

LAYOUT PAPER:

White floral patterned

SUPPLIES:

⅜"-wide green hand-dyed silk ribbon

5¼" circular floral frame

Adhesive foam dots

Beige & orange velvet flowers

Clear vellum

Floral border stickers

Scrap of dark pink cardstock

Small circle punch

Vintage cards

White thread

Easter 1941

BACKGROUND PAPER:

White floral patterned

LAYOUT PAPERS:

Light purple cardstock

Yellow vellum

SUPPLIES:

¼"-wide yellow organdy ribbon

Acid-free tape

Adhesive foam dots

Cream cardstock

Decorative border template

Easter-themed die-cuts

Embossed pewter stickers

Light purple brads

Light purple mulberry paper

Yellow pastel chalk

Easter

Easter this year was quite bittersweet. My grandfather had just received his orders to report to Florida for the US Navy. He was activated for nine months, but was able to return in December, with the end of the War. If you look closely, you can see the service banner in the windows.

—April 24, 1941

DETAILS:

- (above) To create the journaling, print it on the cream cardstock. Wrap a piece of ribbon around the top-right corner of the journaling, securing it on the back side with acid-free tape.

- Using the pastel chalk, highlight selected words in the journaling.

- Mat the journaling onto a torn piece of mulberry paper. Adhere the matted journaling on the first page.

TIP If the original photograph is a Polaroid and the white borders will not fit with your layout, scan and use a photo-editing program to crop the photograph. Be certain not to crop an original Polaroid since this will ruin the photograph.

Spring 1951

BACKGROUND PAPER:

Multicolored block patterned

SUPPLIES:

1" circular word tags

Adhesive foam dots

Cardstocks: light green, peach

Clear vellum

Multicolored striped paper

Punches: large square, medium rectangle

DETAILS:

- To create the mini frames, punch squares from the cardstocks and striped paper.
- Punch out the interior of each square with the rectangle punch.

TIP For this layout, the photographs were taken from colored slides. Using my scanner, I was able to copy the slides to make prints. If you don't have access to this type of scanner, most film shops can do it for you. They can usually do any type of slide or even old negatives. If you have colored slides, you'll notice that the colors don't fade nearly as fast as with most prints.

Father's Day 1975

BACKGROUND PAPER:

Sage green cardstock

LAYOUT PAPER:

Floral embossed vellum

SUPPLIES:

Adhesive foam dots

Alphabet stamps

Black ink pad

Dragonfly stickers

Father's Day card

Kraft cardstock

Mini gold brads

Quote die-cuts

Sage green paper

Tan linen thread

Tan raffia

Vellums: clear, sage green

White mulberry paper

DETAILS:

- (above right) To create the card pocket, secure a torn piece of sage green vellum to the second page with the brads.
- Stamp the word "CARDS" onto a strip of kraft cardstock.
- Pierce (2) small holes on both sides of the stripe.
- Thread linen thread through the holes. Wrap the thread ends around the brads.

Fathers Day

We bought my grandpa a Siberian Hedge plant for Fathers Day. Sagi and I helped him plant it (Sagi just dug the holes!). After we were done, we had dinner, and then posed for pictures. I am so lucky to have these pictures-Grandpa passed away just two years later. He was a great man and I miss him very much.

-1975

The love of flowers is really the best teacher of how to grow and understand them.

HI GRANDPA! HAPPY FATHER'S DAY

CARDS

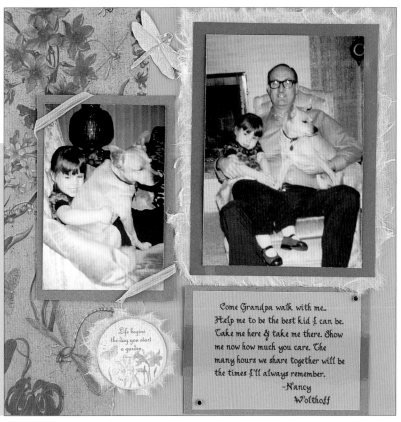

Life begins the day you start a garden.

Come Grandpa walk with me. Help me to be the best kid I can be. Take me here & take me there. Show me now how much you care. The many hours we share together will be the times I'll always remember.

-Nancy Wolthoff

Easter Excitement

BACKGROUND PAPER:

Multicolored block patterned

SUPPLIES:

1½"-wide multicolored plaid wire-edged ribbon

Adhesive foam dots

Circular metal-edged vellum tags: 1½", 2"

Clear vellum

Green brads: mini, regular

Mini orange eyelets

Multicolored striped tags

Stickers: alphabet, Easter egg, number, word

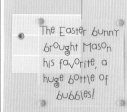

DETAILS:

- (above right) To create the title, spell out "EASTER 2002" with the alphabet and number stickers.

- Place the "E" on a 1½" circular metal-edged vellum tag. Attach an eyelet to the tag and tie a piece of ribbon through the eyelet. Secure the tag to the page, using an adhesive foam dot.

- Apply the remaining stickers to finish the word.

- Print "EXCITEMENT" on a piece of vellum. Carefully tear around the word and layer it on top of the "2002." Secure it in place with the green brads.

July Fun

BACKGROUND PAPER:

Red textured cardstock

LAYOUT PAPER:

Blue textured cardstock

SUPPLIES:

3¼"x4½" decorative frame

26-gauge gold wire

Adhesive foam dots

Alphabet beads

Alphabet stamps

Black ink pad

Die-cuts: patriotic children,
polka-dot alphabet

Gold magic wand charm

Mini gold brads

Patriotic-themed photo corners

Scrap of white cardstock

DETAILS:

- (above right) To create the title, spell out "FOURTH" with the beads. String the beads on a piece of wire. Attach (2) brads to the top of the first page. Secure the beaded wire by wrapping the wire ends around the brads.

- Stamp "THE" above and "OF" after the beaded wire.

- Using the alphabet die-cuts, spell out "JULY" to finish the title. Secure the die-cuts to the top of the journaling, using adhesive foam dots.

The first 4th of July of the new millennium was also Mason's first 4th. We had a BBQ at our house and invited the family over for food, fun and fireworks. Mason loved watching the flashing lights, and Justine & Colter loved lighting (with daddy's help) smoke bombs!

-July 4th 2000

Celebrating
the Fourth

BACKGROUND PAPER:

White speckled patterned

LAYOUT PAPERS:

Patterned: blue star, red swirl

SUPPLIES:

24-gauge silver wire

Acid-free tape

Adhesive foam dots

Alphabet template

Black journaling pen

Cardstocks: navy blue, red, white speckle patterned

Craft knife

Medium star punch

Mini brads: navy blue, red

Mini red eyelets

(designed by: Liz Taylor)

DETAILS:

- To accent each page, punch (3) blue and (3) red stars from the cardstocks. Mat the stars onto the white speckle patterned cardstock. Attach an eyelet to the top of each star.

- Thread a piece of wire, twisting the wire ends near the tops of the stars. Hang the wires over the top of both pages, securing them on the back sides with acid-free tape.

- To create the title, trace and cut out each letter from the red and navy cardstocks. Double-mat each letter with the white speckle patterned cardstock. Adhere each letter in place.

The Fourth of July

BACKGROUND PAPER:
Red cardstock

LAYOUT PAPER:
Blue block patterned

SUPPLIES:
Eyelet words
Silver brads
White cardstock

DETAILS:

- To add the borders to the pages, carefully tear the patterned paper approximately in half. Adhere a half to each page.
- Align the photographs down the left-hand side of both pages.

TIP Consistent placement of the journaling or photographs creates a rhythmic pattern for the page layout.

(designed by: Lesha Dalebout)

October

BACKGROUND PAPER:

Apple patterned

SUPPLIES:

1¾"-square brass frame

Acid-free tape

Berry stickers

Brass studs

Brown fibers

Cardstocks: textured
dark brown, mustard

Clear vellum

Green velvet leaves

Joy charm

DETAILS:

- Create a mat for the photograph by carefully tearing a piece from the mustard cardstock to ½" larger than the photograph.
- Mat the photograph in the center of the cardstock.
- Wrap the fiber twice around the top of the matted photograph, securing it on the back side with acid-free tape.
- Adhere the charm on top of the fibers.

TIP Studs are an excellent way to secure larger or bulkier items to your page. They have (4) prongs, so just about anything will stay in place. Just remember to use a sturdy piece of paper, and to fold the prongs in on the back side.

Harvest Moon

BACKGROUND PAPER:

Tan textured cardstock

LAYOUT PAPER:

Brown checkered

SUPPLIES:

Adhesive foam dots

Autumn-themed die-cuts
(including borders)

Brown buttons: medium, small

Clear vellum

Event memorabilia

Maize cardstock

Off-white thread

Tan mulberry paper

DETAILS:

- As an alternative to adhering
  the journaling to the page,
  secure it by placing a die-cut
  under a button and stitching it
  in the center of the journaling.

- Adhere a border die-cut to the
  top of the journaling.

- Secure another die-cut, using
  an adhesive foam dot, to the
  bottom of the journaling.

Autumn Bliss

BACKGROUND PAPER:

Green plaid patterned

LAYOUT PAPER:

Autumn patterned

SUPPLIES:

½"-wide orange satin ribbon

5"x7" decorative frame

Acorn die-cut

Adhesive foam dots

Autumn-themed stickers

Brown fibers

Oh, the glory of this autumn day,
When the trees unfold their gold!
Oh, how lifted is my spirit,
When such beauty I behold!
Like precious coins, each leaf
holds on through sunshine,
fog, or haze; the memory of
this rich display will warm
My winter days.
-Helen Kitchell
Evans

DETAILS:

- To accent the page, carefully tear the plaid patterned paper in (2) pieces, so approximately 2½" of the background paper shows near the bottom of the page. Adhere the pieces in place.

- Pierce (5) holes, 3" apart, in the plaid patterned paper, just above the background paper.

- Pierce another (5) holes, 3" apart, on the bottom section of the plaid patterned paper, directly in between the previously punched holes.

- In an exaggerated zigzag pattern, thread a piece of fiber through the holes.

Halloween Carnival

BACKGROUND PAPER:

Black cardstock

LAYOUT PAPER:

Purple striped

SUPPLIES:

Black brads

Clear vellum

Kraft cardstock

Wires: 18-gauge purple,
26-gauge silver

DETAILS:

- To draw attention to the journaling, pierce holes in the corners of the mounted piece.

- Thread the 18-gauge purple wire through the top-right hole and back through the top-left hole.

- Twist the wire ends together. Curl the excess wire.

- Repeat the process with the bottom holes.

- To accent the page, curl (2) pieces of the 18-gauge purple wire.

- Pierce holes in the desired positions. Place the curled wire on top of the holes.

Halloween Carnival

Our annual PTA carnival was held on October 2001. I made Mason a dinosaur costume. He loved it! Colter was easy this year-I just had to buy him the CORRECT Batman (believe it or not, there are three different Batman's)! The carnival was a great success and a lot of fun for the kids. Especially when Grandpa Val rode the train with Colter (three times)!

Fun in the Snow

BACKGROUND PAPER:
Red cardstock

LAYOUT PAPER:
Pink polka-dot patterned

SUPPLIES:
¼"-wide white organdy ribbon
Acid-free tape
Black journaling pen
Cardstocks: pink, white
Clear vellum
Mini silver eyelets
Punches: flower, snowflake, star
Rhinestones

The first real snow we got was at the end of November. I bundled Claire up so she could play while I shoveled the driveway. It took her a minute to get used to it, but then she wouldn't come in. The snow came up to her thigh but she insisted on making new trails. She wouldn't go in the same place twice, always walking in the fresh snow. The only reason she came back inside was because one of her boots fell off. November 30, 2001

(designed by: Liz Taylor)

DETAILS:

- (right) To create the left-hand side of the second page, tear (2) ½"x12" strips each from the patterned paper and pink cardstock. Overlap a piece of patterned paper and a piece of cardstock together so that the cardstock barely shows. Repeat with the other (2) pieces.

- Attach each doubled strip to the page with the eyelets. Set the eyelets so that they alternate down the inside edges of the strips.

- Thread the ribbon through the eyelets. Secure the ribbon ends on the back with acid-free tape.

Snow Day

BACKGROUND PAPER:

Red speckle patterned

LAYOUT PAPER:

Black snowflake patterned

SUPPLIES:

Acid-free glitter

Adhesive foam dots

Black journaling pen

Blue pastel chalk

Red brad

Snowflake charm

Snowman die-cut

White artist paper

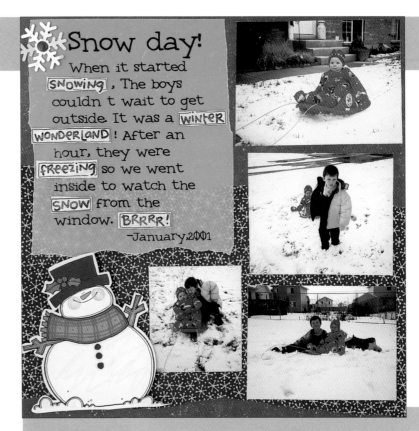

Falling Snow

BACKGROUND PAPER:

Snowflake patterned

LAYOUT PAPER:

Blue

SUPPLIES:

1½"-wide blue organdy ribbon

2" circular metal-edged vellum tag

Alphabet beads

Mini silver brads

Snowflake charm

White fiber

White thread

Winter-themed stickers

Wire word

Merry & Bright

BACKGROUND PAPER:

Black speckle patterned

LAYOUT PAPER:

Red textured cardstock

SUPPLIES:

Acid-free tape

Brads: mini silver star, mini white

Clear vellum

Eyelet word

Ribbons: ¼"-wide red feather-edged, ⅓"-wide green pleated

Tags: 1"-square metal-edged vellum, metal word

White cardstock

White rub-on words

(designed by: Liz Taylor)

Hills' Christmas Portrait

BACKGROUND PAPER:

Red plaid patterned

LAYOUT PAPER:

Holly patterned

SUPPLIES:

⅝"-wide black gingham ribbon

3"x5" decorative paper tag

7"x5" decorative frame

Adhesive foam dots

Black gingham patterned paper

Border template

Christmas-themed die-cuts

Christmas-themed stickers

Clear vellum

Mini candy cane charms

Mini gold brad

Watch face

Word eyelet

Christmas 2000

BACKGROUND PAPER:

Cardstock: green, red

LAYOUT PAPER:

Cardstock: green, red

SUPPLIES:

2"-wide holly print wire-edged ribbon

Cream cardstock

Cream embossed vellum

Mini red brads

Small square punch

Word eyelet

DETAILS:

- (above right) To add the journaling in the layout, print it on the cream cardstock. Cut around the journaling and place it on the page. Secure the journaling to the page by punching (2) square holes at the top of the journaling and threading a piece of ribbon in one hole and back through the other.

- Style the ribbon ends in the front.

- Attach a word eyelet in the center of the ribbon.

merry

Christmas 2000
We had lots of fun preparing for Mason's first Christmas. Lucky for us. while shopping. Justine spied Santa. It's a family tradition for the kids to have their picture with Santa. so we stood in line for 30 minutes! It was worth it even if the kids forgot what to ask him for! As for Mason. he was going through a major stranger anxiety problem—No way would he come within 50 feet of poor Santa! On Christmas day. the kids had a great time playing with all of their new toys. Mason was so overwhelmed. but he was excited. Later in the day. we went to Mardee's for our annual party. We had a great time just relaxing with our family. We are truly blessed! Merry Christmas!

believe

wish

Cowgirl Justine

BACKGROUND PAPER:

Cowboy patterned

SUPPLIES:

1½"-wide red & blue plaid satin ribbon

Adhesive foam dots

Brass star eyelets

Brown pastel chalk

Cardstocks: red, tan

Small circle punch

Stickers: cowboy boots, cowboy hat

Tan linen thread

Vintage images

White artist paper

DETAILS:

- To create a decorative mat, cut the red cardstock to ½" larger than the second photograph.

- Punch circles ⅜" apart around the red cardstock. The holes need not be perfect, but you can mark where you want them on the back side of the frame.

- Using the linen thread and embroidery needle, whipstitch all around the edges. (Refer to Stitches Guide on page 126.)

TIP The importance of a photograph can be enhanced by size, embellishments, and placement.

The Zoo

BACKGROUND PAPER:

Brown cardstock

LAYOUT PAPER:

Multicolored striped

SUPPLIES:

26-gauge silver wire

Alphabet rubber stamps

Animal paper clips

Beads: alphabet, small orange

Black ink pad

Brown pastel chalk

Brown thread or embroidery floss

Clear vellum

Off-white cardstock

Orange brads

Square metal-edged tags: 1", 1½"

DETAILS:

- (above) To create the journaling panel, cut a piece from the off-white cardstock approximately ¼" larger than the journaled vellum.

- Use a decorative stitch around all edges of this piece. If you are hand-sewing, use a blanket stitch. (Refer to Stitches Guide on page 126.)

- Adhere the cardstock piece to the page and place the journaling on top of it.

- To attach the animal paper clips to the page, start by piercing small holes where you want the clips to be placed. Pull the wire through the holes and add a few beads. Then wrap the wire around the animal paper clips and the journaled animals names to hold them in place. Note: Be careful not to tear the vellum.

Cherry Hill

BACKGROUND PAPERS:

Textured patterned: orange, orange & white floral

LAYOUT PAPER:

Lime green textured patterned

SUPPLIES:

Adhesive foam dots

Buttons: lime green, orange

Clear vellum

Embroidery flosses: lime green, orange

Foam flowers: large, small

Cherry Hill

Every year we get season passes to Cherry Hill. The little kids love the pirate ship, while the big kids can't get enough of the waterslides. Angie, Darci, and I just love to sit in the sun and watch the kids.
                                    -Summer, 2003

Mason

Taylor & Colter

Darci, Abby and Angie

Abby the little fish

Justine & Abby

DETAILS:

- To accent the large foam flowers, pierce holes around all the inside edges. Using the backstitch and orange embroidery floss, stitch through the pierced holes. (Refer to Stitches Guide on page 126.)

- To accent the small foam flowers, make one stitch, using the lime green embroidery floss, from the center to the tip of the petal.

- Stitch a colored button in the center of each flower.

- Secure the flowers in place, using adhesive foam dots.

TIP When stitching, you need not worry about your stitches being perfect. The idea is to look "handmade."

Swimming Lesson

BACKGROUND PAPERS:

Patterned: blue block, blue polka-dot

SUPPLIES:

26-gauge blue plastic-covered wire

Alphabet beads

Blue vellum

Brads: blue, seafoam

Pastel chalks: dark blue, light blue

White artist paper

DETAILS:

- (right) To make the memorabilia pocket, cut a piece of vellum and attach it to the page with the seafoam brads. Attach journaling to the pocket with the blue brads.

- String the alphabet beads with a piece of the wire. Curl the excess wire ends. Adhere the wire to the journaling.

- Carefully apply a small amount of chalk between the colored brads and the journaling.

TIP Use the (2) colors of blue pastel chalk to highlight each individual's name.

Pinewood Derby

BACKGROUND PAPER:

Blue cardstock

LAYOUT PAPER:

Yellow striped

SUPPLIES:

Adhesive foam dots

Blue thread

Clear vellum

Event memorabilia

Latex paint samples:
(3) shades of blue

Mini light blue eyelets

Yellow fibers

DETAILS:

- (right) To make the memorabilia pocket, cut a 4½"x10" piece from the yellow striped paper. Cut directly down the center of the piece.

- In the center of the left-hand piece, adhere a paint sample. Layer a scrap of journaling over the paint sample, and using a straight stitch, sew it in place. (Refer to Stitches Guide on page 126.)

- Fold down the top two inside corners of the patterned pieces and secure them in place with the eyelets.

- Attach four eyelets, straight across from each other, in the center of the two striped pieces.

- Thread a piece of fiber through the four eyelets. Sew the striped pieces to the page.

Oklahoma
Wildlife Refuge

BACKGROUND PAPER:

Olive green cardstock

LAYOUT PAPERS:

Brown mesh

Cardstocks: cream, orange

SUPPLIES:

Alphabet metal punches

Cream fibers

Eyelets: brown, orange

Hammer

Silver metal tags: oval, rectangle

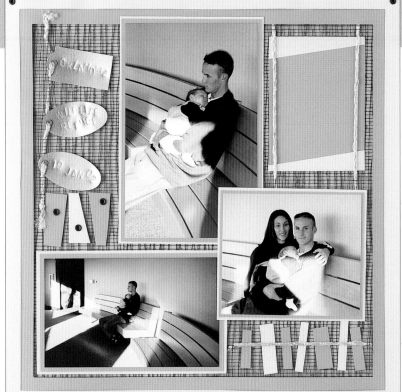

(designed by: Jennifer Leiker Robinson)

The Groundbreaking

BACKGROUND PAPER:

Sage green textured cardstock

LAYOUT PAPER:

Tan textured cardstock

SUPPLIES:

1⅞"x2⅞" decorative paper tag

18-gauge red wire

Adhesive foam dots

Alphabet stamps

Bamboo skewer

Button die-cut

Clear vellum

Gold cardstock

Green raffia

Small square punch

White vellum

Read for the Gold

BACKGROUND PAPER:

Red textured cardstock

LAYOUT PAPER:

Blue textured cardstock

SUPPLIES:

Acid-free tape

Adhesive foam dots

Alphabet template

Award medallion

Gold eyelets

Gold fibers

Gold patterned paper

Gold star charm

Gold star nail heads

Medium star punch

Mini gold brads

White textured cardstock

DETAILS:

- (above right) To keep the medallion in place, secure the ribbon ends on the back side of the page, using acid-free tape.
- Using the brads, attach a photograph over the top half of the medallion's ribbon.
- Attach (2) brads on either side of the medallion and thread a piece of gold fiber around them.

✷ Read for the ✷

To celebrate the 2002 winter Olympics, Midland Elementary held a reading contest. "Read for the Gold" was held from February to March, with the final celebration being a parade around the block, complete with city officials cheering on the kids. While we were parading, one of the kids noticed our cat, Stanley, stuck in a tree! Luckily the fire department was already there, so they rescued Stanley, and everybody cheered! The school photographer snapped a picture of the event, which went into the yearbook! Go for the gold indeed!

March-2002

BBQ

BACKGROUND PAPER:

Orange cardstock

LAYOUT PAPER:

Blue floral patterned

SUPPLIES:

Acid-free tape

Adhesive foam dots

Barbeque-themed die-cuts

Brads: blue, green, orange

Clear vellum

Orange snowflake yarn

Scrap of green patterned paper

Small flower punch

DETAILS:

- To coordinate the pages together, cut (2) 2"x12" strips from the blue floral patterned paper. Adhere a strip the left-hand side of the first page and the remaining strip to the right-hand side of the second page.

- Wrap a piece of yarn vertically around each patterned strip. Secure the yarn ends to the back side of the pages with acid-free tape.

- Punch flowers from the cardstock and a scrap of green patterned paper. Layer the flowers together and attach them to the yarn with the green and orange brads.

- Secure die-cuts to each of the patterned strips, using adhesive foam dots.

Hill AFB Family Day

BACKGROUND PAPER:

Light purple cardstock

LAYOUT PAPER:

Blue speckle patterned

SUPPLIES:

Adhesive foam dots

Alphabet rubber stamps

Alphabet stickers

Black ink pad

Blue fibers

Blue pastel chalk

Large silver eyelets

Silver star brads

Tags: 1¼" circular metal-edged vellum, 1½" circular green, 1½" circular white

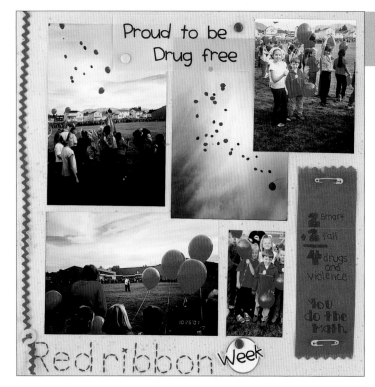

Red Ribbon Week

BACKGROUND PAPER:

Yellow patterned

SUPPLIES:

1¼" circular metal-edged vellum tag

Alphabet stickers

Brads: red, yellow

Clear vellum

Event memorabilia

Mini gold safety pins

Red embroidery floss

Red rickrack

Yellow button

Some Dude's Playground!

BACKGROUND PAPER:

Green cardstock

LAYOUT PAPER:

Yellow cardstock

SUPPLIES:

Alphabet beads

Clear vellum

Mini silver brads

Red cardstock

Red raffia

Silver eyelets

DETAILS:

- (right) To accent the second page, layer pieces of red and yellow cardstocks and adhere them in the center of the page.
- Using the beads, spell out "FUN." String the beads on a piece of raffia.
- Place the bead word on top of the layered cardstock.
- Secure the raffia ends to the page with the brads.

TIP Use bright active colors in the layout to emphasize the photographs.

Kaizilla

BACKGROUND PAPER:

Green checkered

LAYOUT PAPERS:

Cardstocks: green textured, red

SUPPLIES:

Adhesive foam dots

Clear vellum

Gold eyelets

Mini gold brads

Oriental-themed sticker

Paper crimper

Red fibers

Kaizilla

When Kaira was first born, daddy and Kaira would cuddle up on the couch and watch Godzilla movies together. Now they play "Kaizilla"! Daddy uses Kaira's toys to build "Tokyo" & Kaira has fun destroying the city. Daddy even taught her how to roar!

• Arrival in Tokyo •

• Destroy the city •

DETAILS:

- To create the page borders, cut a ½"x12" strip and (2) 12"x1" strips from the red cardstock. Crimp all the strips in the paper crimper.

- Attach the (2) 12"x1" crimped strips on the top and bottom edges of the first page with the eyelets. Thread pieces of red fibers along each strip and through the eyelets. Tie the fiber ends at the corners of the page.

- Carefully tear a 1½"x12" strip from the green textured cardstock. Adhere it to the right-hand edge of the second page.

- Attach the red ½"x12" crimped strip on top of the green strip with the eyelets. Thread pieces of fiber along the strip and through the eyelets. Tie the fiber ends at the corners of the page.

• Daddy roars •

• Kaizilla roars •

• Devour the fallen city! •

The Park

BACKGROUND PAPER:

Pink textured cardstock

LAYOUT PAPER:

Pink striped

SUPPLIES:

Acid-free tape

Assorted shaped and sized decorative tags

Clear vellum

Decorative border template

Light pink rickrack

Mini orange rivets

Washer words

Yellow textured cardstock

The **Park**

On a sunny Saturday in March, we took Kaira to the park for the first time. She loved to play on the slide and loved to be pushed on the swings. Luckily the park is right next to grandma Mardees, so we can come as often as we want!

—March 13th 2004

DETAILS:

- Loop pieces of rickrack around the top and bottom of a washer word.

- Attach the rickrack ends and the washer word on the first page with the rivets.

- Secure the other end of the rickrack on the back side of the pages, using acid-free tape.

- Loop another piece of rickrack around another washer word. Hang the piece over the top edge of the second page.

- Attach the rickrack end and the washer word on the second page with a rivet.

- Secure the other end of the rickrack to the back side, using acid-free tape.

Justine's Dance Competition

BACKGROUND PAPER:

Purple cardstock

LAYOUT PAPER:

Black cardstock

SUPPLIES:

1¼" circular metal-edged tag

2"x⅞" metal nameplate

26-gauge silver wire

Acid-free tape

Adhesive foam dots

Alphabet rubber stamps

Alphabet stickers

Black ink pad

Clear vellum

Event memorabilia

Flower brads

Mini pinwheel

Mini silver brads

Purple fibers

Purple pastel chalk

Silver journaling pen

Justine & Colter

BACKGROUND PAPERS:

Cardstocks: pale gold, off-white

SUPPLIES:

⅞"-square silver metal buckle

1½"-wide tan satin ribbon

5"x4" decorative frame

Adhesive foam dots

Button & lace border stickers

Clear vellum

Die-cuts: butterflies, flower, quote

Gold flower eyelets

Off-white thread

Rub-on alphabet

Tan journal patterned paper

Tan pastel chalk

Pink Justine

BACKGROUND PAPER:

Light pink textured cardstock

LAYOUT PAPER:

Dark pink textured cardstock

SUPPLIES:

Adhesive foam dots

Alphabet rubber stamps

Black ink pad

Clear vellum

Mini pink safety pin

Mini silver brads

Multicolored embroidery floss

Multicolored medium buttons

Multicolored striped paper

Pink rickrack

Rub-on word

Silver word embossed tags

Stickers: alphabet, word, flower, polka-dot border

DETAILS:

- Mat the photograph to the patterned paper and adhere to the page.
- Attach the pink rickrack to the page by securing it on the back side with tape.
- Apply the flower and word stickers on top of the rickrack. Secure the alphabet sticker with an adhesive foam dot.

The First Time
I Saw the Ocean

BACKGROUND PAPER:

Crumpled-paper patterned

SUPPLIES:

1"-square orange tags

1⅞"x3⅝" decorative tag

Adhesive foam dots

Clear vellum

Confetti fiber

Craft knife

Mini silver brads

The first time I saw the ocean, I thought of the endless water, the blue sky, and all of the fish inside.
—Colter Hill
April 2002

Santa Monica pier

DETAILS:

- To secure one of the photographs in place, use a craft knife to cut (2) slits in the page—vertically 1" apart and ¼" wider than the photograph. Slide the photograph through the slit.

Slide Fun

BACKGROUND PAPER:

Green cardstock

LAYOUT PAPER:

Yellow checkered

SUPPLIES:

Alphabet rubber stamps

Black ink pad

Metal alphabet charms

Yellow buttons

Yellow fiber

(designed by: Liz Taylor)

Learning to sLidE head first is much more FuN than sitting

May 9, 2002

Ocracoke Island

BACKGROUND PAPER:

White cardstock

LAYOUT PAPERS:

Cardstocks: blue textured, light blue, periwinkle

SUPPLIES:

Acid-free tape

Beach-themed embellishments

Clear vellum

Cream fiber

Mini silver brads

DETAILS:

- To create the background, use the white cardstock for the scrapbook page.

- Crop the variety of blue cardstocks onto different sizes to create the color-block effect. Adhere each piece onto the white cardstock.

- To coordinate the pages, string pieces of fiber horizontally across each page. Secure the fiber ends to the back side of the page, using acid-free tape.

(designed by: Sherri Wright)

We Love to Camp

BACKGROUND PAPER:

Orange textured cardstock

LAYOUT PAPER:

Purple textured cardstock

SUPPLIES:

22-gauge plastic-covered wires: orange, purple

Brads: mini dark pink, orange, purple

Clear vellum

Mini orange eyelets

Multicolored striped paper

Paper crimper

Purple pastel chalk

White artist paper

We love to

CAMP!

We took the kids to weber canyon for an overnight campout, Masons first! Justine & Colter loved to catch "water skeeters" in the river & Mason just loved being outside. At night, we roasted marshmallows and told silly stories. We love to camp!

-July 24th 2001

DETAILS:

- To coordinate the pages, cut (2) 12"x1" strips from the purple textured cardstock and adhere them near the top edge of each page.

- Attach orange brads to the ends of each purple strip.

- Crimp (2) 12" pieces of orange plastic-covered wire in the paper crimper.

- Secure the wire piece to each purple strip by wrapping the ends around the orange brads.

Camping

BACKGROUND PAPER:

Brown textured cardstock

LAYOUT PAPER:

Leaf patterned vellum

SUPPLIES:

Alphabet stickers

Brown brads

Bone folder

Cardstocks: dark sage green, off-white

Craft knife

Punches: large square, medium square, small leaf

Trip memorabilia

Twine

DETAILS:

- To place the vellum on the page, apply adhesive to just the edges. Cut a 4¼" horiztonal slit where the journaling panel will be positioned.
- Cut a 4¼"x7½" piece from dark sage cardstock.
- From top edge of piece, cut 2¾"x6¾" rectangle.
- Cut ¼" off the rectangle's sides and bottom.
- Lightly sand the edges of both pieces.
- Place rectangle in the middle of ardstock piece.
- Adhere both pieces to the vellum piece, just below the slit.

TIP The artist collected leaves from her trip and laminated them in plastic.

(designed by: Jennifer Leiker Robinson)

THANKSGIVING POINT

children's

In celebration of the end of chemo and claire's picc line removal, grandma barb took us to thanksgiving point. It took claire and garrett a few minutes to get used to the idea that they could get wet. After that they both splashed around and played next to "Noah's Ark". We couldn't get them to come out of the water until they were both so cold their lips were blue & they were shaking. What a fun outing with grandma barb! ☺

(designed by: Liz Taylor)

BACKGROUND PAPER:

Red cardstock

LAYOUT PAPER:

Oatmeal cardstock

SUPPLIES:

Alphabet stickers

Animal charms

Black journaling pen

Cream thread

Medium square punch

DETAILS:

- (above) To accent the bottom portion of the page, punch (5) squares from the oatmeal cardstock—cut the sixth one slightly larger than the others.
- Line the squares along the bottom edges of the page, positioning the largest square third in from the left.
- Adhere all the squares in place.
- Adhere a small photograph on the larger square.

water gardens

August 2002

Bear World

BACKGROUND PAPER:
Multicolored plaid patterned

LAYOUT PAPER:
Green cardstock

SUPPLIES:
Brass eyelets
Clear vellum
Die-cuts: bear, bear paws, trees

DETAILS:

- (above) To accent the left-hand side of the first page, carefully tear a strip from the cardstock. Adhere the bear paw die-cuts to the piece and attach eyelets between them.

TIP Make sure you know the placement of each piece before you tear the paper. This way you will be certain not to tear too much or not enough.

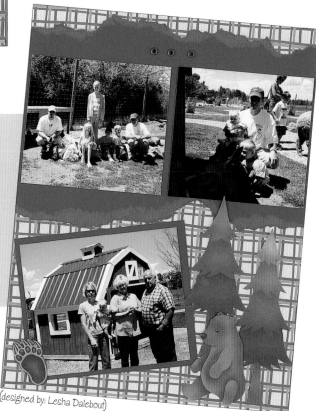

(designed by: Lesha Dalebout)

The Robinson Family 2003

BACKGROUND PAPER:

Blue cardstock

LAYOUT PAPER:

Kraft cardstock

SUPPLIES:

Black journaling pen

Bone folder

Cardstocks: brown, dark brown, green, white, yellow

Pastel chalks: brown, orange

Seashell stickers

Small circle punch

DETAILS:

- (right) To make the tree, tear a large piece from brown cardstock for the tree trunk and adhere it in place.

- Tear (7) leaves from green cardstock. Using the bone folder, make a leaf pattern on the back side of the leaves. Adhere each leaf to the tree truck.

- Tear (3) coconuts from the brown paper. Punch (9) small circles from the dark brown cardstock. Adhere (3) circles to each coconut.

- Layer the coconuts on the middle of the leaves and adhere them in place.

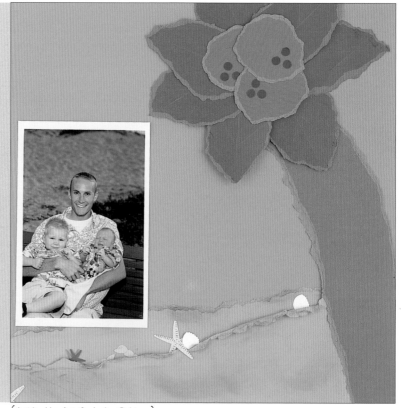

(designed by: Jennifer Leiker Robinson)

Moments of Solitude

BACKGROUND PAPER:

Fishing-themed patterned

LAYOUT PAPER:

Green leaf patterned

SUPPLIES:

3"-wide tan mesh ribbon

Adhesive foam dots

Brown fibers

Clear vellum

Fishing-themed die-cuts

Gold eyelets

Mini gold brads

Rub-on words

Stickers: alphabet, fishing-themed

Tan rickrack

A Mad River

BACKGROUND PAPER:

Multicolored striped

SUPPLIES:

Adhesive foam dots

Alphabet stamps

Alphabet stickers

Black ink pad

Clear vellum

Multicolored fibers

Purple brads

Purple eyelets

Tags: 2"-square, 2¼" circular

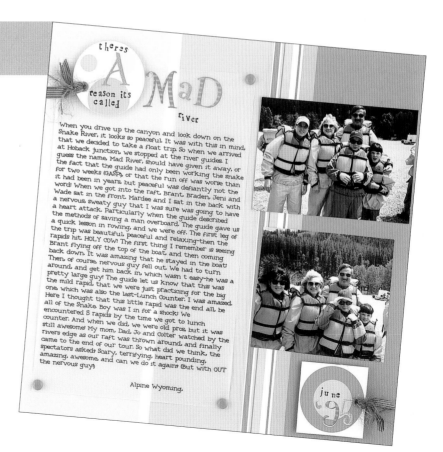

Lagoon

BACKGROUND PAPER:

Blue textured cardstock

LAYOUT PAPERS:

Blue journal patterned

Lime green

Multicolored striped

SUPPLIES:

Adhesive foam dots

Assorted mini colored brads

Assorted sized buttons:
blue, red, yellow

Light green thread

Stickers: alphabet, numbers

Our favorite things about WHIRL LAGOON

Mason loved riding "Budgies", the log flume, the planes with dad, and puff the little dragon. Colter loved it when Brant won him a snake. Justine just liked looking for cute boys, and Mom, grandma and Mardee just had fun watching it all!

June 28th

2003

DETAILS:

- (above) To create the journaling, print it on the vellum, leaving enough space between the title and the rest of the journaling to fit the stickers. Adhere the journaling in place on the first page.

- Finish the title and add the date, using the stickers.

- To create interest, attach a colored brad to each sticker.

BACKGROUND PAPER:
Black cardstock

LAYOUT PAPER:
Beige floral patterned

SUPPLIES:
Beige brads
Cardstocks: beige, cream
Clear vellum
Fibers: black, white
Musical score die-cut

DETAILS:

- To accent the page, tear (2) pieces from the patterned paper.

- Place the smaller piece under the journaled title and adhere it to the page. Attach (2) brads to the patterned piece. Thread pieces of fiber around the brads.

- Place the larger piece vertically on the second page. Alternate the brads down the left and right sides of the piece and thread the fibers in a zigzag pattern across to each brad.

(designed by: Breanna Berntsen)

Our Travel Journal

SUPPLIES:

½"-wide green hand-dyed silk ribbon

1"-square metal-edged vellum tag

Adhesive

Alphabet rubber stamps

Alphabet stickers

Alphabet tiles

Black ink pad

Charms: key, lock

Travel images

Watercolor journal with elastic band fastener

DETAILS:

- To make the title, spell out "OUR" with the tiles. Adhere them in place over the top image.

- Spell out "TRAVEL" with the stickers. Apply them under the top image.

- Stamp "JOURNAL" near the bottom of the journal cover.

- Remove the center from the tag.

- Attach the lock charm to the tag with a piece of ribbon.

- Adhere the tag on the cover so that it is framing the stamped word.

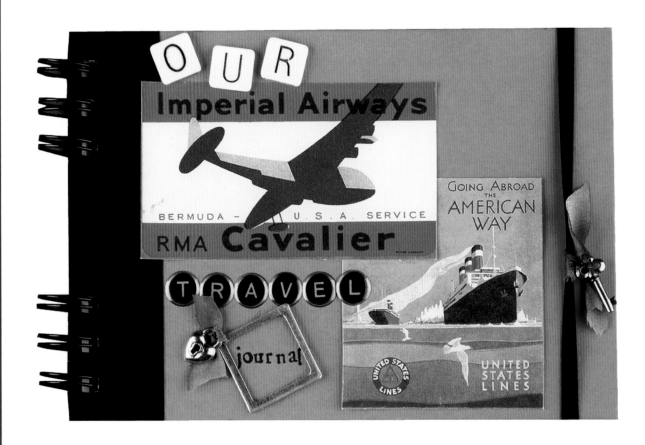

Graduation Journal

LAYOUT PAPER:

Cream journal patterned

SUPPLIES:

¼"-wide black gingham ribbon

½"-wide black journaled twill ribbon

2¼" oval metal nameplate

2¼"-square metal frame

Adhesive foam dots

Black fibers

Clear vellum

Clock die-cut

Mini silver snaps

Number eyelet

Spiral-bound journal

Stickers: alphabet, ribbon

Graduation Card

BACKGROUND PAPER:

White cardstock

LAYOUT PAPERS:

Cardstocks: brown, pumpkin, sienna

SUPPLIES:

Bone folder   Tan cardstock

Jute

DETAILS:

• Cut (2) 3"x6" strips from the tan cardstock. Loosely roll the strips and secure with the jute. Adhere them to the front cover.

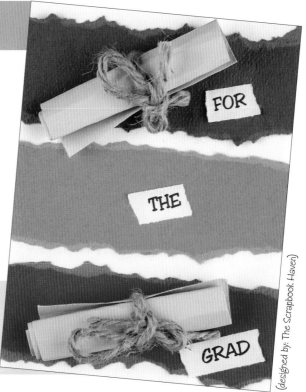

(designed by: The Scrapbook Haven)

Wedding Card

BACKGROUND PAPER:

White cardstock

LAYOUT PAPERS:

Light green

Pink floral patterned

SUPPLIES:

½"-wide light green & white striped satin ribbon

Adhesive foam dots

Bone folder

Brads: large silver, mini silver

Cake die-cut

Clear vellum

Green & pink silk flower

Pink acid-free glitter

Small square punch

White tulle

DETAILS:

- To create the card cover, cut a 2¼"-wide piece from the pink patterned paper to the length of the card. Use a straight stitch to secure the piece to the center of the card. (Refer to Stitches Guide on page 126.)
- Tear a 2½"-square piece from the light green paper.
- Cut a similar-sized square from the tulle and layer over the left-hand side of the light green piece.
- Stitch both pieces in place near the bottom-right corner.
- Secure the die-cut on top of the tulle piece, using an adhesive foam dot.
- Accent the card with the journaling and silk flower.

New Baby Card

BACKGROUND PAPER:
Light pink textured cardstock

LAYOUT PAPER:
Pink journal patterned

SUPPLIES:
1¼"x3¾" decorative tag
Bone folder
Clear vellum
Pink chenille rickrack
Pink embossed border paper
Pink thread
Rub-on word
Silver brads: large, mini
Washer word

Party Favor Pinwheel

PROJECT PAPERS:
Multicolored striped
Pink embossed cardstock

SUPPLIES:
¼"-wide pink paper ribbon
¼"-diameter wooden dowel
1"x4¼" decorative tag
Alphabet stamps
Black ink pad

Flower sticker
Large yellow button
Lime green brad
Purple eyelet
White acrylic paint

Birthday Gift Box

PROJECT PAPERS:

Textured cardstocks: green, pink

White artist

Yellow embossed

SUPPLIES:

Bone folder

Box template

Clear vellum

Dry-embossing tools

Flower brass-embossing template

Ribbons: ¼"-wide green organdy, ¼"-wide yellow variegated, 1½"-wide pink sinamay

Rub-on word

Silver eyelet

Birthday Card

BACKGROUND PAPER:

White textured cardstock

SUPPLIES:

¼"-wide yellow woven ribbon

Adhesive foam stars

Balloon charms

Mini red eyelets

Red fibers

Rub-on words

Washer word

Friendship Card

BACKGROUND PAPER:

Multicolored striped

LAYOUT PAPER:

Green floral patterned

SUPPLIES:

2½"-square silver metal frame

Bone folder

Large silver eyelets

Pink thread

Ribbons: ½"-wide green & pink hand-dyed silk, 3"-wide cream mesh

Stickers: buttons, floral, photo corners

White cardstock

Vintage image

Mini Book

COVER PAPER:

Striped linen patterned

SUPPLIES:

1¼" circular metal-edged vellum tag

1¾"x½" metal nameplate

Adhesive foam dots

Brown fibers

Card-sized scrapbook kit

Gold eyelets

Jute

Mini silver brads

Off-white linen thread

Rub-on words

Silver button rivets

Stickers: numbers, stamp

Valentine Card

BACKGROUND PAPER:

Red cardstock

LAYOUT MATERIAL:

Scraps of fabric: heart patterned, red checkered

SUPPLIES:

⅛"-wide red polka-dot ribbon

⅓"-square mini silver

½"x3" beige decorative tag

Adhesive foam dots

"B" alphabet charm

Black photo corners

Black thread

Mini red brads

Red fibers

Red & white striped string

Rub-on alphabet

Stickers: alphabet, valentine

DETAILS:

- Cut a piece of the heart fabric and sew to the front of the card.
- Thread the buckle through the ribbon and fasten the ribbon to the card with the mini brads.
- Apply the alphabet stickers on the ribbon.
- Secure the Valentine sticker, using an adhesive foam dot.
- Place the photo corners in each corner of the card.

Easter Egg Hunt

BACKGROUND PAPER:

Off-white artist

LAYOUT PAPER:

Multicolored striped

SUPPLIES:

1½"-wide plaid wire-edged ribbon

Bone folder

Brads: purple, mini teal

Clear vellum

Small square punch

Stickers: Easter-themed, word

DETAILS:

- To make the card, cut a 5"x11" piece from artist paper. Score and fold the piece horizontally in half.

- Punch (2) squares near the top of the fold.

- From the backside, thread the ribbon through both squares. Pull the ribbon ends through to the front of the card and style.

- To create the interior of the card, cut the journaling and a piece of striped paper to 4"x5".

- Apply a sticker in the center of the striped paper.

- Align the journaling over the striped paper and attach both pieces to the interior of the card with mini teal brads.

Mother's Day Book

COVER PAPER:

Green floral patterned

INTERIOR PAPER:

Pink floral patterned

PAGE PAPERS:

Striped: green, pink

SUPPLIES:

⅝"-wide green hand-dyed silk ribbon

Bone folder

Card-sized scrapbook kit

Clear vellum

Floral sticker nameplate

Heart charm

Mini silver brads

Rhinestones

Silver spiral paper clips

Threads: pink, white

White paper flower

Wired pink hydrangea petals

DETAILS:

- Use the templates from the scrapbook kit to create the book cover, and the pages from the patterned and striped papers.

- To attach the journaling to the pages, use the paper clips. Adhere rhinestones to the edge of the journaling to secure it.

- To attach the pages to the cover, thread the ribbon over the folded page crease and around the spine. Secure the ribbon by tying a bow on the spine.

TIP As an alternative to adhesive, stitch the pages together, using a straight stitch. (Refer to Stitches Guide on page 126.)

Father's Day Card

BACKGROUND PAPER:

Kraft cardstock

LAYOUT PAPERS:

Patterned: green textured, multicolored plaid

SUPPLIES:

Adhesive foam dots

Black embroidery floss

Jute

Mini black eyelets

Tag punches: large, medium

White paper

(designed by: The Scrapbook Haven)

DETAILS:

- To make the card, cut a piece of the kraft cardstock 8½"x 5½". Score in the middle and fold.
- Set (2) eyelets near the bottom of the card. Thread the jute through the eyelets.
- Punch the large tag from the kraft cardstock and the medium tag from the green. Adhere them together.
- Set an eyelet in the hole, and attach the jute.
- Journal on the white paper and adhere to the tag.
- Secure the tag to the card, using adhesive foam dots.

Halloween Card

BACKGROUND PAPER:

Gray artist

LAYOUT PAPERS:

Patterned: black dot,
orange plaid

SUPPLIES:

2¼"x1½" metal-edged vellum tag

2½"-wide orange webbed ribbon

Adhesive foam dots

Alphabet eyelets

Alphabet stamps

Black fibers

Black ink pad

Bone folder

Halloween-themed acrylic tokens

Mini orange rivet

Orange thread

Witch sticker

DETAILS:

- To create the card, cut a piece of the gray artist paper to 10"x5½". Score directly down the center, and fold.
- Cut the patterned papers to fit the card. Tear down the right-hand side of the plaid patterned paper. Using a zigzag stitch, stitch the polka-dot patterned paper to the left-hand side of the card. (Refer to Stitches Guide on page 126.)
- Layer the ribbon on the cut edged of the plaid patterned paper. Center and zigzag stitch both pieces to the card.
- Attach the tag with the rivet and alphabet eyelet.
- Thread the fibers through the tokens and attach, using the adhesive foam dots.

Christmas Card

BACKGROUND PAPER:
Red textured cardstock

LAYOUT PAPER:
Red polka-dot patterned

SUPPLIES:
½"-wide black gingham ribbon
Black fibers
Black thread
Envelope template
Large brass flower eyelets
Small brass hinges
Small daisy appliqué
Small word eyelet tag
Vintage image

DETAILS:
- Use the envelope template to create the card. Trace and cut the card from both the patterned paper and the textured cardstock. Stitch the pieces together, using a straight stitch. (Refer to Stitches Guide on page 126.)
- Attach an eyelet on the flaps.
- Attach the vintage image to the interior of the card, using the hinges.
- Add your personalized greeting under the vintage image.
- Tie pieces of ribbon through the eyelets to close the card.
- String a piece of the fiber over the envelope.
- Tie the fiber ends to appliqué and tag.

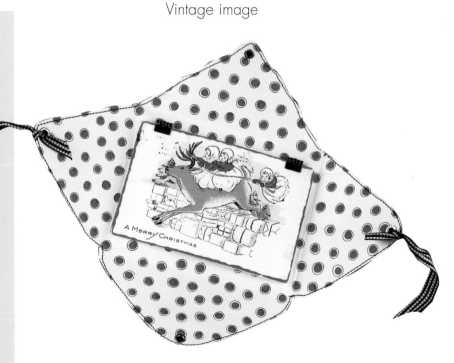

Stitches Guide

The stitching done on the projects can be done with a sewing machine. If you choose to sew by hand, following you will find instructions for the required stitches.

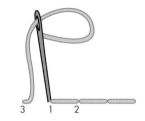

Bring needle up at 1. Go down at 2. Come up at 3. Go down at 1.

BACKSTITCH

Bring needle up at 1. Go down at 2. Come up at 3, looping thread under needle. Continue for length of stitching, keeping needle vertical.

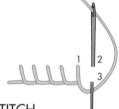

BLANKET STITCH

CROSS STITCH

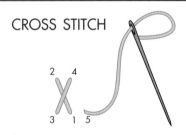

Bring needle up at 1. Go down at 2. Come up at 3. Go down at 4. To create another "X", bring needle up at 5, etc. All top stitches should lie in the same direction.

This stitch may be taut or loose, depending on desired effect. Bring needle up at 1. Go down at 2 upon achieving desired length.

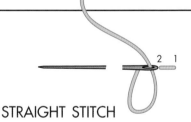

STRAIGHT STITCH

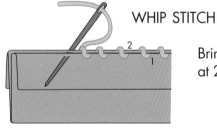

WHIP STITCH

Bring needle up at 1. Whip thread over and go down at 2. Repeat until pattern has been established.

This stitch is done with a back and forth movement. Bring needle up 1. Go down 2. Come up 3. Go down 4.

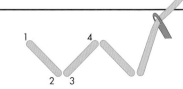

ZIGZAG STITCH

About the Author

PAIGE WAYMENT HILL

I have always been a creative soul. As a child, one of my favorite activities was creating something. Whether decorating for the holidays or helping my mom with pinecone wreaths, something artistic was always going on.

In college, I worked in retail sales and studied fashion merchandising. That is where I met my future husband and his beautiful 2-year-old daughter Justine. We were soon married, and a short time later, Colter was born. Six years later, we had our little Mason.

Along the way, I have been in business with my parents, teaching craft classes, and selling handcrafted items to gift and interior stores. I enjoy sewing, tole painting, interior design, and, of course, scrapbooking. However my favorite thing of all is my family: whether camping, hiking, playing, or just relaxing at home, there is no place I'd rather be.

Thanks to all my wonderful family and friends! I love you all. I hope you enjoy the layouts in this book, and can take inspiration from the ideas.